GRACE COOLIDGE:
SUDDEN STAR

(A VOLUME IN THE PRESIDENTIAL WIVES SERIES)

OTHER BOOKS IN THE PRESIDENTIAL WIVES SERIES

Dolley Madison
Paul M. Zall
2001. ISBN 1-56072-930-9. (Hardcover)
2001. ISBN 1-56072-937-6. (Softcover)

A "Bully" First Lady: Edith Kermit Roosevelt
Tom Lansford
2001. ISBN 1-59033-086-2. (Hardcover)
2003. ISBN 1-56072-648-8. (Softcover)

Sarah Childress Polk, First Lady of Tennessee and Washington
Barbara Bennett Peterson
2002. ISBN 1-59033-145-1. (Hardcover)
2002. ISBN 1-56072-551-1. (Softcover)

Frances Clara Folsom Cleveland
Stephen F. Robar
2002. ISBN 1-59033-245-8. (Hardcover)
2004. ISBN 1-59454-150-7 (Softcover)

Lucretia
John Shaw
2002. ISBN 1-59033-349-7. (Hardcover)
2004. ISBN 1-59454-151-5 (Softcover)

Betty Ford: A Symbol of Strength
Jeffrey S. Ashley
2003. ISBN 1-59033-407-8(Hardcover)
2004. 1-59454-149-3 (Softcover)

Grace Coolidge:
Sudden Star

Cynthia D. Bittinger

Nova History Publications, Inc.
New York

Copyright © 2005 by Nova Science Publishers, Inc.

All rights reserved. No part of this book may be reproduced, stored in a retrieval system or transmitted in any form or by any means: electronic, electrostatic, magnetic, tape, mechanical photocopying, recording or otherwise without the written permission of the Publisher.

For permission to use material from this book please contact us:
Telephone 631-231-7269; Fax 631-231-8175
Web Site: http://www.novapublishers.com

NOTICE TO THE READER
The Publisher has taken reasonable care in the preparation of this book, but makes no expressed or implied warranty of any kind and assumes no responsibility for any errors or omissions. No liability is assumed for incidental or consequential damages in connection with or arising out of information contained in this book. The Publisher shall not be liable for any special, consequential, or exemplary damages resulting, in whole or in part, from the readers' use of, or reliance upon, this material.

This publication is designed to provide accurate and authoritative information with regard to the subject matter covered herein. It is sold with the clear understanding that the Publisher is not engaged in rendering legal or any other professional services. If legal or any other expert assistance is required, the services of a competent person should be sought. FROM A DECLARATION OF PARTICIPANTS JOINTLY ADOPTED BY A COMMITTEE OF THE AMERICAN BAR ASSOCIATION AND A COMMITTEE OF PUBLISHERS.

LIBRARY OF CONGRESS CATALOGING-IN-PUBLICATION DATA
Grace Coolidge: Sudden Star / Cynthia D. Bittinger
      p. cm.
Includes index.
ISBN 1-59454-473-5 (hardcover)

Published by Nova History Publications,
New York

For My Precious Four

Bill, Kate, Aimee, and Will

CONTENTS

Foreword		ix
Preface		xi
Acknowledgments		xv
Chapter 1	Sudden Star: The New First Lady	1
Chapter 2	Growing Up in Vermont	5
Chapter 3	Teaching and Marriage	13
Chapter 4	Northampton Years	21
Chapter 5	Heading to the National Stage	37
Chapter 6	The White House Years	53
Chapter 7	Retirement from Public Life and Death of the 30th President	97
Chapter 8	"Precious Four" and Life on Her Own	107
Bibliography		123
About the Author		127
Index		129

FOREWORD

The old saying that "behind every successful man is a woman" is perhaps nowhere more evident than in the White House. Even a cursory examination of the wives of presidents reveals a group of remarkable individuals who made many contributions to the lives and careers of their husbands, the presidency, and even the nation. Over the course of U.S. history first ladies have presided over state dinners, overseen extensive historical renovations of the Executive Mansion, held press conferences, campaigned for their husbands, testified before Congress, championed important social causes, and addressed the United Nations.

As a candidate for the presidency speaking of the role his wife would assume in his administration Bill Clinton stated that when the public elects a president, they are getting "two for the price of one!" To an extent such a statement has always been true. First ladies have been a viable part of the presidency since the nation's founding. Of the men who served as president during the country's history, nearly all of them served with a first lady at their side. Only a handful of presidents have held the office without their spouses. For instance, both Andrew Jackson and Chester A. Arthur had lost their wives prior to their presidencies; Rachel Jackson dying in the interim between her husband's election and his inauguration and Ellen Arthur just prior to her husband's Vice Presidency. The wives of both Thomas Jefferson and Martin Van Buren passed away years before their presidencies. But they were exceptions. Only two bachelor presidents have been elected, Grover Cleveland and James Buchanan, however the former married while in office. Three presidential wives died while serving in the White House: Letitia Tyler, Caroline Harrison, and Ellen Wilson. However, both President John Tyler and President Woodrow Wilson later remarried while in office.

Presidential wives have served without pay and, until very recently, often without proper recognition. So too have they wielded political power and social influence despite the fact that they are neither elected nor appointed. In part because they are not elected or accountable to the citizenry and in part because of strict social conventions that precluded women from participating in politics for much of the nation's history, presidential wives have been forced to exercise their power and influence in a behind-the-scenes manner. Yet, in this capacity many wives have functioned as their husband's trusted confidante and private political advisor.

Presidential wives have faced great challenges, not the least of which include the loss of privacy and specter of assassination looming for themselves and their families. The presidency is arguably the most demanding job in the country and the challenges of the office are experienced by the president's family. Amazingly, several first ladies served while trying to raise a family. Presidential wives have faced severe scrutiny, an invasive press corps and curious public, and criticism from journalists and the president's political enemies. This is perhaps one of the experiences that all first ladies have shared. Not even popular wives like Martha Washington, Abigail Adams, or Jacqueline Kennedy were spared from harsh personal attacks.

The first ladyship has been the "unknown institution" of the White House. For most of its history it has been ignored by scholars and overlooked by those studying national and presidential politics. However, this is slowly changing. The public, press, and scholars are beginning to take note of the centrality of the first lady to the presidency. A new view of the president's spouse as a "partner" in the presidency is replacing more traditional views of presidential wives. Even though the Founding Fathers of the country gave no thought to the president's wife and the Constitution is silent concerning her duties, today the "office" has become a powerful, recognized institution within the presidency, complete with staff and budgetary resources that rival the so-called "key" presidential advisors.

The first ladyship is one of the nation's most challenging and dynamic public offices. So too is it an office still in development. In the words of First Lady Barbara Bush, concluding her remarks when delivering the commencement speech at Wellesley College, "And who knows? Somewhere out in this audience may even be someone who will one day follow in my footsteps, and preside over the White House as the President's spouse. I wish *him* well!"

In the volumes of this Series the reader will find the stories of women who fashioned the course of American history. It is the goal of the publishers and myself that this book and each volume in the Presidential Wives Series shed light on this important office and reveal the lives of the women behind the American presidency. I hope you enjoy this book and the entire Series!

Robert P. Watson, Series Editor

PREFACE

Grace Anna Goodhue was an only child. Her parents doted on her and gave her every advantage they could. They were upwardly striving, but definitely middle class Vermonters. In turn, Grace was very devoted to them and constantly looked out for their welfare. Yet she still had a yearning to understand the world and take joy in whatever the world might offer. Her college education widened her horizons; her goal of teaching deaf children to speak gave her a challenge.

When she began the adventure of a marriage with a rather silent, strong minded man, she had no idea that they would ever live in the White House. She did not plot or plan for it. On the contrary, she cared for their two boys at home in Northampton while her husband traveled to Boston for a week of politics returning only for the weekends. She did not become part of Calvin's political life until they moved to Washington and he held a national office.

Grace Coolidge was an important balance to her husband. He was known for being shy and quiet, yet he chose a political career to please his father. He forced himself to reach out and meet strangers even though it was always hard for him. When he met Grace Goodhue in 1904, he found a soul mate to soothe him, as well as someone who could make others comfortable in social settings. In those days, however, women stayed home and did not generally involve themselves in political matters, especially in a public way. Once Calvin and Grace started a family, Grace had a reason to stay home: to take care of their children. Thus Calvin circulated in political circles and climbed the political ladder in Massachusetts on his own. Grace remained at home and became the center of the family. She raised the boys with little interaction from their busy and often preoccupied political father.

Both family life and political life were changed because of Frank Waterman Stearns. Stearns, the political mentor who met Coolidge when he was President of the State Senate, saw the potential of Grace Coolidge. She was the one who had magnetism and could entertain in Boston and help the rising political star, her husband. Calvin Coolidge turned down this proposal since it would mean moving to Boston and disrupting his family life, along with adopting a life style he could not afford. Coolidge wanted to live within his means. He did not want to be beholden to anyone. Thus Grace's political contributions would come much later. Not until Calvin was Vice President in 1921, did the Second Lady emerge as a fashion trendsetter, cordial social mixer, and the one who remembered names and faces—a great political asset. She was a positive force for his career. Now Calvin could be himself – thoughtful and funny -- and his wife would handle the social life. Grace was a traditional woman and she was new to the Washington scene. Her husband had been a governor, not a U.S. Senator or Cabinet member, so she diligently followed protocol when she arrived.

At the White House, Grace followed a rather boisterous first lady, Florence Harding, who had reached out to the public very effectively. The White House grounds and building were reopened to the public by the Hardings. Grace and Calvin felt they could not retreat on this; they wanted to keep the openness of the Harding administration. Grace came to call herself the "national hugger." Florence Harding had spontaneously greeted the public, even offering tours of the White House. Grace preferred a schedule where she would pose with visitors for photographs at twelve noon on the stairs. She brought back holiday traditions as a national role model. Easter egg rolling, lighting the Christmas tree, shaking hands on New Year's Day were special events for the public. She supervised the White House staff in a world of transition. Her first housekeeper went to market in a horse drawn carriage! Her second one traveled by automobile. Grace, as first lady, was to manage a very large White House staff after being a mother in Northampton with a single housekeeper. She was to stretch to manage people in a pleasant way even though her husband occasionally meddled in household affairs. He wanted to know how many hams were bought for a dinner since he had to pay the bill. At that time a president paid for food for his family, staff, and guests. Other expenses came from an entertainment and operations budget. Just as Edith Roosevelt supervised renovations of the White House so did Grace, even donning a hard hat one day to inspect the changes in the third floor, the family residence.

In an era of jazz dancing and high living, Grace Coolidge chose a very proper role. She and Calvin restored dignity to the White House after the poker-playing, drinking days of the Hardings. She also had to keep her head up as scandals were revealed about the former Harding administration. She and Calvin were to rise above all of that and earn the trust of the American people. In 1924, Calvin Coolidge was re-elected and continued to be popular throughout his presidency.

Grace Coolidge endured a most tragic death of a family member in front of the nation's eyes. She, just like Jacqueline Kennedy in modern times, was the model of decorum and helped the nation accept the death of a younger son since he would be going to the "great everlasting." She took immense joy in the life of her remaining son. She was a mother and wife during a time when society was challenging this kind of moral, upright life.

Grace found the strain of the White House a burden as did her husband. It was hard to be perfect all the time, and they were constantly in the public eye with the media covering every move. Every decision was important. When their time in office was over, Grace was content to be a citizen again just as Calvin was. She did not use her public recognition for anything except fund raising for what she considered very important causes such as the education of deaf children. She preferred to travel "under the radar screen."

She kept her modest lifestyle and ethical values and her devotion to family. Her head was never turned away from responsibilities or ways she could help, whether it was in the capital of the nation or in the town of Northampton, where her volunteer activities, in later years, filled her days with purpose. She decided to help preserve her husband's history in Plymouth Notch, Vermont and managed property there during the depression and World War II.

This short book is to provide readers with an overview of Grace's life and her time in Washington. Her own values, as seen through her personal letters, form the new material for this book. She cared about friends, family, and community. She was moved by nature to take in the world with all her senses. She wanted to make each person she met feel special. She was disappointed that she could not teach her husband the joy of play. However, she did not dwell on what could have been. She took what life gave her and made the most of it!

She was a first lady who tried not to comment on her husband during his lifetime, but she made one important effort to correct the public's picture of him after his death. She asked fifty people he had worked with to write short articles for *Good Housekeeping* magazine. She added her own anecdotes and shared her last love letter from her husband with the editors. Her charming comments warmed up the image of her husband and his presidency.

Since Grace Coolidge lived twenty four years longer than her husband, she had a long and productive retirement. Grace was a dutiful grandmother and loving friend. It meant a great deal to her that a group of Smith College graduates accepted her in their Northampton group. Finally her intellectual capacities were appreciated, but she made sure the group had fun! She devoted herself to community projects and always took joy in making the smallest difference. Her warm smile cheered up boys going off to war. In whatever she did, she showed her concern for others.

Grace Coolidge was a private person. Her articles on her life in magazines in the 1930's represented her public side. Her private letters written to friends and relatives over many years showed her personal side. She never knew historians would read them. I have mined the letters for insights and hope this book will be beneficial to those studying first ladies and women in American history.

ACKNOWLEDGMENTS

Robert P. Watson had the inspiration to create this series. He also had faith that I, a first time author, could write this book. For this I am grateful. The Calvin Coolidge Memorial Foundation accepted the project with enthusiasm even though they knew that I would need time for research and writing. Jerry Wallace was a willing and thoughtful guiding light on this project. With him as my coach, I could find the way. Tordis Ilg Isselhardt was a thoughtful, insightful editor.

The Coolidge family is to be thanked for saving and making available the letters which I have read to research the story of Grace Coolidge. I interviewed the late John Coolidge and found him always willing to discuss his mother whom he adored. Lydia Coolidge Sayles shared all the information she had and tried to support me in any way she could. After her death, her husband, Jerry Sayles, donated 200 letters to build the Calvin Coolidge Memorial Foundation's Archive. Dartmouth College and Edward Connery Lathem donated letters from Grace Coolidge to Ivah Gale. Jean Hoskison donated letters from Grace to her parents to the Coolidge Foundation. Jennifer Sayles Harville, John Sayles, and Christopher Coolidge Jeter will now be the ones to help us interpret and recount the history of their family.

Coolidge experts over the years tutored me in what to look at and how to evaluate it. The late Lawrence Wikander, curator of the Coolidge Room at Forbes Library, was indispensable in all things Coolidge. His co-editor Robert H. Ferrell has opened my eyes to research and continues to do so. The "Coolidge underground" with notables such as historian Sheldon Stern and interpreter Jim Cooke has opened up new avenues of research.

Several repositories have been essential. Forbes Library, Amherst College, Historic Northampton, Edwards Church, the Vermont Division for Historic Preservation, the Vermont Historical Society, the Pi Beta Phi archives, Smith College, Mercersburg Academy, and the Calvin Coolidge Memorial Foundation

(CCMF) archives were the source of letters and research materials. Fran Becque, archivist of Pi Beta Phi, should be singled out for her assistance. Bill Jenney, site administrator for President Calvin Coolidge State Historic Site, shared Grace's letters to White House housekeeper Ellen Riley. I have learned so much from the writings of Ishbel Ross, Robert Ferrell, Claude Fuess, Edward Connery Lathem, and Gloria Stoddard. The volunteers who wrote articles for the *Real Calvin Coolidge* booklet are important for their contributions.

Mimi Baird, Howard Coffin, and Karen Mansfield helped facilitate donations of letters by Grace Coolidge to CCMF which enhanced this book greatly. Calvin Coolidge Memorial Foundation Board members from 1990 to 2004 have patiently urged me to research and write. Their enlightened attitude has made an important difference. CCMF executive directors from 1970 to 1990 managed to improve the archives with limited resources.

Funding is always critical. An anonymous foundation sent funds to help underwrite the project. Senators Robert T. Stafford and James M. Jeffords found support for CCMF's preservation and education efforts.

Vermont Public Radio aired my commentaries on the Coolidge family. Betty Smith skillfully edited the work, which then garnered a Vermont Associated Press award and recognition from the American Association for State and Local History.

One cannot write a book without family support. My precious four were always there cheering me on. My friends from college days were also there to listen and encourage the project.

The story of Grace Coolidge, a wonderful woman and memorable first lady, should be told. She once said her letters would be worthless to save for their financial value since she wrote so many. Her letters were the real story; their value is priceless.

Chapter 1

SUDDEN STAR: THE NEW FIRST LADY

"Mrs. Coolidge received the delegates of the Pi Beta Phi conference yesterday afternoon, April 11, at 4:30 o'clock at the White House on the occasion of the presentation of a portrait of Mrs. Coolidge, who is a Pi Beta Phi. The portrait, which was painted by Mr. Howard Chandler Christy, and will be hung in the White House, was received in the east room by Lieut. Col. Clarence O. Sherrill, superintendent of public buildings and grounds."[1]

Friday, April 11, 1924 was one of Grace Coolidge's happiest days at the White House. Her husband, President Calvin Coolidge, was pleased with the public acceptance of his policies, and seemed assured of being nominated and elected President in his own right that coming November. Their sons were doing well at Mercersburg Academy in Pennsylvania. The President's father, Col. John Coolidge, who had just turned 79, was enjoying his son's success up in Plymouth, Vermont. Her mother, Lemira Goodhue, whose health was fragile, was adjusting to her new life after moving into the Coolidges' two family house in Northampton, Massachusetts from her home in Burlington, Vermont.

This event took place nine months after the Coolidges moved to the White House upon the startling death of President Warren Harding. He and his wife, Florence, had been on a Western tour, taking them across the country to the West Coast and up to Alaska. He had kept up a hectic pace of speech-making and public appearances despite having a heart condition. The Vice President, Calvin Coolidge, was with Grace on his father's farm at Plymouth Notch, Vermont, when word came of Harding's unexpected death on August 2, 1923. Suddenly, the

---

[1] Jozy Dell Hall, White House Days, extractions from *The Washington Post*,(Washington: privately printed for the Coolidge family, 1931) p. 37.

young couple was thrust into the spotlight. Grace Coolidge, the new first lady, was a sudden star.

Pi Beta Phi Fraternity visits the White House, April, 1924 (Pi Beta Phi archives)

When she became the Second Lady upon her husband's inauguration as Vice President in March of 1921, she was under intense scrutiny. Since Mrs. Harding was the wife of a Senator, she already knew the ways of Washington when she became the first lady. Grace Coolidge, coming from Massachusetts, had found her unofficial office all very new and daunting. Without a governor's residence in Boston, she had done very little entertaining in her state's capital. She had stayed at home in western Massachusetts without her husband to raise their two sons.

As the new first lady, she quickly found her footing. She continued social activities that Florence had initiated, but did not immerse herself in politics as Florence had willingly done. Grace looked to the traditions that were in place and took advantage of the newly voted-in government budget for entertaining.

This new first lady would preside over the White House in the golden era of the 1920's. It was a wonderful and exciting time. The new jazz music, brought into almost every home by the modern technology of radio, set the pace. Americans, anxious to move on with their lives after World War I, focused on business and pleasure. Government and politics did not matter much to them. Stories of heroes, royalty, crime, and murder were front page news. New fashions were all the rage, with the well dressed flapper looking to Hollywood's movie stars not European royalty for cues. Hemlines were rising. Grace Coolidge's sense of style would serve her in good stead. "It took her only a short time to find her bearings with the parade of diplomats and judges, of Senators and financiers, of newspaper owners and railroad czars, of doctors and scientists, of writers, artists and musicians, of celebrities from all parts of the world who now moved into her sphere."[2]

During the two weeks she spent packing to move into the White House from the New Willard Hotel, she had thought about possible new traditions that could be adopted. The sickly atmosphere at the White House of the Wilsons and the sleazy crowd of the Harding days would be replaced with a joyful family and a wife and mother who wanted to express her affection for the American people.

That April of 1924 the Pi Beta Phi's Eastern Conference would be held at the White House. It turned out to be the largest gathering of fraternity women ever convened with a total of 1,350 representing every state.[3] The Pi Phi's were welcomed through the east entrance of the White House and assembled to form a semi-circle "about the panel on the west wall, where hung the curtains, in wine red velvet, with cords of silver blue, which covered the portrait." A presentation party gathered, the Marine Band began to play, aides to the president from the Army, Navy, and Marines escorted Grace Coolidge to the room. "She wore a soft grey georgette crepe afternoon dress trimmed with crystal, and as jewels, a diamond eagle on her shoulder, a chain with a crystal pendant, a gold bracelet, her wedding ring, and the diamond studded arrow which had been presented the day before by a group of personal friends in Pi Beta Phi."[4] The portrait was presented "as an expression of its pride and affection" since Grace Goodhue Coolidge "has brought honor to her fraternity, not only through the distinguished position which she now fills so graciously and so well, but also through her life which has ever made apparent her faithfulness to the pledges of loyalty, service, and noble womanhood made by her to Pi Beta Phi."[5]

The portrait of Grace Coolidge was painted by Howard Chandler Christy, a portraitist of the elite including politicians and prominent businessmen. In the painting, the First Lady stands on the White House lawn with Rob Roy, the President's white collie, by her side. Her brilliant red velvet evening gown is enhanced by a gauze scarf draped at her shoulders. The Michigan and Vermont

---

[2] Ishbel Ross, *Grace Coolidge and Her Era, the Story of a President's Wife* (Rutland, Vermont: Academy Books, 1962) p. 106.
[3] Fran DeSimone Becque, "Grace Coolidge: Pi Beta Phi," *The Real Calvin Coolidge* #17, p. 27. The term sorority came into fashion much later.
[4] Ibid., p. 28.
[5] Ibid., p. 29.

Beta members drew silver blue cords to part the heavy wine-red curtains to unveil the painting. Guests celebrated in the Blue room and gathered in the gardens for a long, magnificent panoramic picture of the women with in various hats and exotic coats of the period. Grace Coolidge, realizing that this day was special, commented to those near her, "This is the loveliest thing I have seen here. I should like to keep you here always, to make beautiful the White House lawn."[6]

This day of April 11th was rather exceptional. Usually functions at the White House centered on her husband and his duties. "Deference to the office" was required.[7] Being the wife of the president "took precedence"; Grace's "personal likes and dislikes must be subordinated to the consideration of those things which were required."[8] Her husband's "first duty" was to the people.[9] Ironically, those who left the ceremony by the front door brushed near four men walking up the north portico. This was the President and his aides returning from his afternoon walk![10]

How did Grace Coolidge become this sudden star on the national scene? This was a very unpredictable outcome for this daughter of an engineer and a homemaker from Burlington, Vermont. Granted, as an only child, she had been given many advantages, but to live in this national realm was quite a reach. How did Grace Coolidge become a sudden star, a beloved first lady of the nation from 1923 to 1929?

---

[6] Ibid, p. 30.
[7] *Grace Coolidge: An Autobiography.* eds. Lawrence E. Wikander and Robert H. Ferrell (Worland, Wyoming: High Plains Press, 1992), p. 62.
[8] Ibid.
[9] Ibid.
[10] Ibid., p. 30.

Chapter 2

GROWING UP IN VERMONT

"The sun, moon, and stars, in the opinion of my parents, revolved about my infant head, and never was a babe more tenderly loved and cared for than I."[1]

When she was born on January 3, 1879, Grace Anna Goodhue was welcomed as a precious gift to her parents. There were to be no other children. She was the apple of their eye.

Her parents, Andrew Issachar Goodhue and Lemira Barrett, both from New Hampshire, had married in their home state in 1870 and traveled to Burlington, Vermont for his job at the Gates' cotton mill. They were living in company housing at 315-317 St. Paul Street, located near the railroad tracks and Lake Champlain, when their daughter was born. Andrew wanted his own home and proceeded, in 1881, to build a house on lower Maple Street where the family lived until Grace's college years.

Lemira Barrett was brought up in Merrimack, New Hampshire by her maternal grandmother. Her own mother had died when she was three years old. She was raised in a "strict New England fashion."[2]

Grace's father was born in Hancock, New Hampshire in 1848; one of six children. At eighteen years of age he traveled to Nashua, New Hampshire to apprentice for three years as a mechanical engineer. It was there that he met his future wife.

He was a descendent of Goodhue settlers from Ipswich, Massachusetts. Grace must have had considerable pride in his family since opening paragraphs in articles on her life began with, "My father, Andrew Issachar Goodhue, was of the seventh generation of a Massachusetts family descended from William Goodhue

---

[1] *Grace Coolidge: An Autobiography*, p. 3.

who came over from England in 1635 and settled in Ipswich."[3] Benjamin Goodhue, a Federalist, was a member of the first U.S. Congress and became a U.S. Senator in 1797. Grace's pioneer relatives ventured forth to Hancock, New Hampshire.

Grace Anna Goodhue as a little girl (Goodhue family album)

Grace Anna Goodhue was born into a vibrant and active city. As now, Burlington was the county seat--30 miles from the state capital and 60 miles from Montreal, Quebec. It was already a college town, home to the University of Vermont, founded in 1791. The downtown, where she was born, overlooks Lake Champlain, the sixth largest lake in the United States. The ferry service on the lake, the train service to the big cities of Boston and New York, made Burlington

---

[2] Ibid, p.2.
[3] Ibid., p.1.

a vital northern urban hub. The booming lumber industry helped the city become a major port in the 1800's. The Vermont dairy industry was growing with railroads carrying their products to other parts of New England and to Quebec. In 1885, there was even a streetcar for urban travel. The horse and buggy era in Vermont was passing, especially in the urban areas.

Grace reminisced later about her life as an only child with "few playmates of my own up until I went to school."[4] Her intense bonding with her mother led to a feeling of obligation that she carried with her until her mother's death. Her mother made clothes for the family and devoted herself to helping others through the church. She "flitted to and fro on errands which proclaimed her love."[5] In photographs of Grace as a young child, she had long auburn hair and a pleasant face. She was a prettier version of her mother.

A vivid memory for Grace was the "tragedy" of her father's injury at the mill when she was only five years old.[6] As he was working, a piece of wood flew into his face and injured his nose, jaw, and eye muscles. To make the home quieter, Grace was to stay with neighbors during this time. She was distressed about her father, but gained a second home from this experience. The Yale family, all three generations, embraced her. She learned to knit from the grandmother and found a role model in June Yale, the older daughter. Grace's visits with the Yales in future years would bring her in contact with deaf children and would set her on a path toward helping similar children.

The only child of an upwardly mobile urban family in America at the end of the 19th century, Grace was offered enriching experiences. As she wrote in her autobiography, "My parents desired that I should have every advantage which they were able to give me, and they denied themselves many pleasures which they might have enjoyed in order that I should have the opportunity to develop any latent talent which I possessed."[7] Her parents bought a piano and arranged for her to take lessons. In high school, she took singing lessons. Music was to become a lifelong interest. She was an active child. She sledded and skated and partook of winter sleigh rides in these early years.

Church and religion were as natural to Grace Goodhue as breathing. She wrote, "I cannot remember the time when I did not attend church. ...I was enrolled in the infant class in Sunday School as soon as a teacher was willing to assume charge of so small a child..."[8] The Methodist Church dominated the social

---

[4] Ibid., p. 5.
[5] Manuscript of Grace Coolidge's Autobiography, Forbes Library, Northampton, Massachusetts, p. 7.
[6] *Grace Coolidge:An Autobiography*, p. 9.
[7] Ibid., p. 21.
[8] Ibid., p. 11.

and religious life of the family; Andrew Goodhue taught Sunday School and was the superintendent. Church was an influential part of Grace's life.[9] When there were "revival services among the Protestant churches of the city," young people went to hear different ministers.[10] So sixteen year old Grace listened to the sermons of a Burlington Congregational minister, Rev. Peter M. Snyder, and changed churches; her parents soon followed. Her father became an important church leader for the College Street Congregational Church just as he had been to the Methodist Church. Her parents were willing to follow her choice so as to be with her in her spiritual journey.

Grace Goodhue had a tremendous rapport with her father. She felt he was "indispensable." She wrote, "As a child I had believed that he could mend my neck if I broke it..."[11] In 1886, Andrew left Kilborn and Gates to build a machine shop with William H. Long. They were manufacturers of steam fire engines, pulp machinery, horse nail machinery and mill supplies.[12] The next year, Andrew, an active Democratic party supporter, was appointed Inspector of Boilers of Steam Vessels for Lake Champlain by President Grover Cleveland. Andrew was probably responsible for the home improvements of a steam furnace and electricity. In 1898, the machine shop was sold but Andrew continued to inspect steam vessels until his retirement in 1920 at the age of 73. He was known as Captain Goodhue and people enjoyed him for his "good fellowship."[13] He was described as a "wealthy local manufacturer" in New England papers.[14] His daughter admired his outgoing personality and his solid protection. He was also fun. He popped corn with her and took her sledding!

The world widened for Grace beyond her parents and their friends when she attended church and also when she started school. She approached school and life as learning experiences where she could meet new people and be open to new ideas. This appears to differ from her mother's very circumscribed idea of growing up female. Luckily both mother and daughter were interested in musical training and an active social life. Grace felt that opportunity came to those who had "early training and environment."[15] She credited the schools of Burlington, Vermont for that essential training. Parents and teachers often knew each other quite well and cooperated in educating the children. Her first teacher, Cornelia

---

[9] Ibid., p. 14
[10] Ibid, p. 23.
[11] Ibid., p. 24.
[12] Ibid., p.18.
[13] Ibid., p. 25.
[14] Northampton newspaper, October 4, 1930, Coolidge family personal files.
[15] Ibid., p. 16.

Underwood, gained her confidence and lifelong devotion. Miss Underwood was able to change Grace's behavior from being rambunctious to being productive.

Grace characterized herself as "not a brilliant student" but even so was a commencement speaker in the June of 1897 and it was assumed by her parents that she would enter the University of Vermont, right up at the top of the hill in her town of Burlington. This was unusual for a woman of her time. It was rarely expected that a woman would seek a higher education or that a family could even afford college for a woman. Grace lived at home during her college years, but her parents nonetheless denied themselves many pleasures to ensure that their daughter would be given every opportunity—opportunities which had not been offered to them when they were young.

Grace Goodhue, as she entered college at age nineteen, was five feet four inches and, as seen in pictures from her college years, had "masses of lustrous dark hair but her eyes were her most remarkable feature. Gray-green, they seemed hazel in certain lights. They were wide-set and grave, even when her face was alight with laughter. ...Her generous mouth gave character to her face, which was strong rather than symmetrical."[16]

Grace began the University of Vermont in the fall of 1897 with the class of 1901, but withdrew less than three months later for two reasons. One was that she needed to improve her health and another was that she was to care for an aunt, the widow of her uncle, Dr. Perley E. Goodhue, who lived in Haverhill, Massachusetts. An oculist (eye physician) had recommended she take time off. Biographer Ishbel Ross noted that Grace had "trouble with her spine as a child but vigorous exercises had strengthened her."[17] Grace definitely liked long walks and made them a lifelong habit each day.

Fortunately, before she left the University of Vermont she befriended Ivah W. Gale of Newport, Vermont in the class of 1901. Ivah was a shy girl from a farm on the shores of Lake Memphremagog and "Grace had observed how lonely and lost she seemed on the college campus" and they became close friends.[18] Once Grace re-entered the university in 1898 with the class of 1902, she invited Ivah to move in with her family in 1900 and in subsequent letters wrote to her as "My dearest beloved sister" or signed off with "a great big hug and kiss from Your Ol'Sis".[19] Ivah was as close as a sister to Grace for the rest of her life. "Totally

---

[16] Ross, p. 4.
[17] Ibid., p. 4.
[18] Ibid., p. 6 and 27.
[19] Grace Goodhue to Ivah W. Gale, Ivah W. Gale Collection, the Calvin Coolidge Memorial Foundation, Plymouth, Vermont.

unlike in every way, we became fast friends and I knew in her the strong ties which often bind together two sisters."[20]

Grace took her studies seriously, but had fun along the way. Grace did not want to be a "5 lark" or a "grind".[21] She was an all around college woman with time for work and also for social life. Ivah wrote, "I believe that any of Grace's college friends would say that she was "full of fun", but it is hard to do justice to that rare quality of her humor because it is her personality that gives it interest and life."[22]

Grace enjoyed college life where they thought up entertainment instead of going to college sponsored events. She wrote in articles on her life that she played Sir Toby Belch in a theatrical production at the university. Her recounting of the play rehearsals includes a certain female student who had fallen "head over heels in love" with Sir Toby.[23] She discounted her popularity on campus but enjoyed the diversions and social life. "Everyone who knew Grace in her college days remembered that she was always ready to sing, or play the piano, or join in a skit."[24] College life was fun for this young woman. She was vice president of her class during her sophomore year and sang contralto in the Glee Club.[25]

According to her friends' recollections, Grace dated in college. Clarence Noyes escorted her to many a church social and became a friend she visited with over the years.[26] Frank Joyner was serious about Grace, but her family "disapproved" of him. She continued to write him after he left Burlington and broke off this correspondence when a more serious suitor came into her life.[27]

Grace must have been thinking about being a teacher, one of the few occupations open to female college graduates. She took her education seriously. "Most of us were there because of a definite plan which we had made for the future, and we were trying seriously to prepare ourselves in accordance with it."[28]

Grace showed leadership qualities when she sought to establish another female fraternity on campus and became its corresponding secretary.[29] She was one of 14 who petitioned for a charter from the national fraternity of Pi Beta Phi and she was often host for the meetings at her home. This was the start of her

---

[20] *Grace Coolidge: An Autobiography*, p. 27.
[21] 5 lark would be a wild person; grind would be a serious, boring studious type.
[22] Ivah Gale Collection.
[23] Ibid., p. 30.
[24] Ross, p. 5.
[25] Ibid., p. 4.
[26] Ibid., p. 6.
[27] Ibid., p. 7.
[28] *Grace Coolidge: An Autobiography*, p. 28.
[29] Term sorority was not used at this time.

lifelong association with the fraternity, often known for cookie shines (a baking party) and public service. As Ivah Gale recalled, "Grace was the life of our fraternity meetings and was always ready to do her share in entertaining the crowd."[30] She wrote a history of the fraternity chapter and sang it to the tune of the song "Nellie Gray." Grace found this all female association to be important to her. After graduation, she was nominated for higher offices in the national organization and found a group of friends for life.

During her college years, Grace's father built a house at 312 Maple Street, very near the university, which was home to the family from 1899 to 1923. The Pi Beta Phi's often held meetings in the attic and Ivah Gale lived there until her graduation and start of her own teaching career.

A professor at the University of Vermont, during Grace's freshman year, had written on her paper entitled "Life" that she "refrain from writing upon this subject until you have had more experience."[31] Perhaps he was being facetious, but Grace did stifle her urge to write for many years. When she again wrote, it was in poetry. She also kept up a steady stream of correspondence with family and friends. In these letters, she commented on what she was doing, but rarely looked back. She looked forward to the next adventure, the next step in getting to know the world around her.

Her education provided her with a familiarity with classical music, theatre, the arts, and literature. Growing up in a city also exposed her to lectures and local theatrical productions. Her courses instilled in her a discipline of how to study which would help her as she tackled the course of life. She was exposed to the urban world of Burlington and to the world of the university with concerts, a museum, gardens, and a life of the mind. She felt she was prepared to receive further training as a teacher. She could impart some of what she knew to others and widen their world.

---

[30] Ivah Gale Collection.
[31] *Grace Coolidge: An Autobiography*, p. 54.

Chapter 3

TEACHING AND MARRIAGE

"What a good girl to tell me so soon how your children were pleased with the pictures. ...I know you have your duties and I want Miss Yale to know you are her best instructor," wrote Calvin Coolidge.[1]

Grace did not forget her early aspiration to teach children with hearing impairment. This was one reason she had attended the University of Vermont. Her goal was to follow the Yale family to the Clarke School for the Deaf in Northampton, Massachusetts. June Yale, a daughter in a neighboring family she had gotten to know well at the time of her father's accident, taught at Clarke, where her aunt Caroline A. Yale was the principal. June married another teacher and moved to Philadelphia. Nevertheless, Grace persisted in wanting to go to Clarke, and wrote Caroline Yale, who offered her a teaching post.

Caroline Yale was a leader in the field of teaching deaf children to speak. She developed vowel and consonant charts which were also used to teach reading as a phonovisual method.[2] Her goal of placing children in the world of people with normal hearing was innovative and copied world wide. Grace not only sought to be near the Yale family but to be instructed by a world class educator.

The Clarke School was known for the "technique of oralism, which trained children in speech and speech-reading."[3] This pioneering school where children would read speech from the lips of others and "be returned as quickly as possible to the ranks of hearing children to complete their education" was chartered by the

---

[1] Cynthia D. Bittinger, "Calvin Coolidge's Courting Letters, 1904-1905," *The New England Journal of History* (1998), p.70.
[2] Cynthia Parsons and Kathleen Whalen, *Eleven Awesome Vermont Women* (Scottsdale, Arizona: The Vermont Schoolhouse Press, 2004), pp.99-104.
[3] Charlene McPhail Anderson, "Grace Coolidge and the Clarke School for the Deaf", *The Real Calvin Coolidge # 10* (1994): p. 1.

Massachusetts legislature in 1867.[4] The school recognized that society's acceptance was important. Barriers could be broken down if a child spoke instead of signing with his hands, a language that few knew at the time.

In 1871, Alexander Graham Bell first came to the Clarke School to teach the faculty his father's method of "visible speech"; he was associated with the school for 51 years. He served on the Board from 1898 to 1922. Dr. Bell referred to himself first and foremost as a teacher of the deaf and not an inventor. It was while trying to develop a practical hearing aid that he came upon the idea for the telephone. Later in life, he married Mabel Hubbard, the daughter of the founder of the Clarke School.[5]

Grace Goodhue taught for three years at the Clarke School. She began her training in the fall of 1902, taught in the primary school, and then in the intermediate school. This difficult work engaged her and she never lost her devotion to the school. She chose a very daunting occupation. Most schools continued to use sign language when she began this work; she was in a small school with few teachers and students; students could not hear and they longed for communication. She must have had many frustrating days. Her sunny, optimistic personality was a joy to her students and their achievements were her reward.

Lemira Goodhue had been reluctant to let her daughter move to Northampton. She had hoped that Grace would teach in the public schools of Burlington after graduation. Her solace was that Northampton "was a woman's town, the seat of Smith College, and she had been told that the few men who lived there were married."[6] Lemira could continue to look for an eligible male for her daughter to marry and one who lived in the Burlington area. She wanted a role in Grace's life, perhaps even to be the one to find a husband for her.

The city of Northampton had been founded around Meeting House Hill and then spread over the surrounding low, rolling hills. The streets went up the hill to Smith College at the western end and Main Street was a wide, impressive boulevard with the Hampshire County Courthouse, the City Hall, the Edwards Church, the Memorial Hall, and the Academy of Music. The city was a trading and industrial center at the turn of the century with about 15,000 of native Yankee stock and some Irish immigrants. Paradise Pond was part of the Smith campus and offered a pleasant walk along its shore up to the Clarke School. Northampton was an educational center with Amherst College, Massachusetts Agricultural

---

[4] Ibid.. p. 6.
[5] Clarke School history, Clarke School for the Deaf website
[6] *Grace Coolidge: An Autobiography*, p. 30.

College, Mt. Holyoke College, Williston Seminary, the Capen-Burnham School and the Clarke School for the Deaf all in town or near by.[7]

Grace Goodhue lived on the campus of the Clarke School in Baker Hall. A young, 32 year old lawyer named Calvin Coolidge rented an apartment across the street. He was a fellow Vermonter, born in 1872, in a very rural area called Plymouth Notch near Woodstock and Ludlow. He had attended a preparatory academy in Ludlow and was an up and coming, hard working young man who was a graduate of Amherst College.

He read the law and clerked in the Northampton firm of Hammond and Field, was admitted to the bar in 1897, and the following year opened his own law firm. He had already waded into the waters of politics as a city councilman, city solicitor, and clerk of the courts for Northampton. When he met Grace he was chairman of the Republican City Committee. Calvin was a slender man with blue eyes, sandy-red hair and a "white, intense face", "good looking" with a "jutting nose both delicate and pointed, a keenly chiseled profile and cleft chin."[8] He was "regarded as a rising young man and an eligible bachelor."[9]

Humor surrounds how they met, but in each of their autobiographies, they failed to describe their first meeting. Others have reconstructed the event. Blanche Brown Bryant, a Coolidge relative, recounted this story she credited to Grace Goodhue Coolidge. "The apartment house where I lived was across the street from the one Calvin occupied. Every morning he stood in the window to shave, with his derby hat on the back of his head. The man who cared for the building I was in was also the janitor for his apartment across the way. We had flowers in a window box, and from it I took a nasturtium plant, put it in a small flower pot, and asked my janitor to deliver it to the young man. The next morning my flower was on the sill of his window. The janitor brought back his calling card with a message asking that he might call."[10] Several biographers recount a similar story with Grace watering flowers and looking up at Calvin seen in his window in his underwear or union suit wearing a hat and Grace breaking out in laughter. Eventually Calvin explained why he shaved with a hat on. An unruly lock of hair got in the way and he plastered it down with a comb "anchoring it firmly with his hat while he washed his face and lathered up."[11] Calvin then noticed Grace outside and asked Robert Weir, his landlord and steward of the Clarke School, to

---

[7] Claude M. Fuess, *The Man from Vermont, Calvin Coolidge* (Boston: Little Brown and Company, 1940), p. 76-77.
[8] Ross, p. 9,11-12.
[9] Fuess, p. 87.
[10] Blanche Brown Bryant, *Calvin Coolidge as I Knew Him* (DeLeon Springs, Florida: The E.O. Painter Printing Company, 1971), p. 15-16.

arrange an introduction. Robert Weir commented on this meeting "that having taught the deaf to hear, Miss Goodhue might perhaps cause the mute to speak."[12] He was referring to the notably quiet, intense lawyer meeting a teacher of the deaf. Calvin had a long history of shyness. All his life he would struggle to meet people and communicate.

Their relationship became more serious. Calvin, in his *Autobiography* written in 1929, recalled, "From our being together we seemed naturally to come to care for each other....We thought we were made for each other."[13] The couple began writing letters to each other in June of 1904 even though they were neighbors and had access to telephones. Biographer Ishbel Ross commented that Calvin did have a crush on another woman before Grace, but according to biographer Fuess, only Grace attracted his attention. Calvin sought advice on dating from Jim Lucey, the cobbler whom he had befriended in college days. Grace conferred with Ivah Gale, her best friend from college. Ivah recalled, "I think he wanted her right off. He worked his way with her."[14] Calvin's courting letters to Grace (hers are not known to be saved), show that he wooed this sprightly, vivacious teacher with many kind words and entreaties. He wrote on November 6, 1904, "Sometimes the best part of having you with me is after you are gone. For it is only when I am alone again that I realize how much pleasure you really made for me and remember that I expressed so little of it to you at parting...if you gave me much practice I might learn to do a little better."[15] Jim Lucey suggested that he compliment her. He did so by writing about how he liked a gown or asked when he could he see a particular white dress again.

Ethel Stevens was not so sure about the romance. When Grace and Calvin visited her, he would not talk and the social situation was awkward. Grace criticized Calvin for this, but his reply was that, "She'll find I'm human."[16] Grace openly admitted that they were "vastly different" in temperaments and tastes.[17] She could enjoy sports, social life and dancing. He had two left feet and preferred to read at night or go to political meetings. His rural Vermont grandmother had brought him up with an avoidance of dancing, drinking, and card playing. Calvin and Grace shared interests were poetry, walking, a love of Vermont, appreciation

---

[11] Ross, p. 9.
[12] Ibid.
[13] *The Autobiography of Calvin Coolidge* (New York: Cosmopolitan Book Corp., 1929) p. 93.
[14] Ross, p. 13.
[15] Cynthia D. Bittinger, "Calvin Coolidge's Courting Letters, 1904-1905," *The New England Journal of History*, p. 70.
[16] Fuess, p. 89.
[17] *Grace Coolidge: An Autobiography*, p. 32.

of flowers, and romance. He wrote, on February 8, 1905, "the star you showed me—shall we see it together again soon?"[18]

Evidently, the courting of Grace by Calvin hit a roadblock when he proposed marriage and mother Lemira discouraged this proposal. Lemira wanted her daughter to return home and learn to bake bread.[19] Lemira relented, but the date of the wedding was still a source of disagreement between the future mother-in-law and son-in-law. Grace recounted, "Mr. Coolidge took the position that we were both old enough to know our own minds, that he was able to support a wife, and that there was no reason to delay. In the course of the debate the wedding date was advanced until Mother held out for November and Calvin October. Eventually he won in the draw."[20] Lemira held onto her daughter as long as she could. Grace's father was more supportive.

On October 1, 1905 Grace Goodhue wrote Ivah Gale, her friend who could not get to the wedding on October 4th. A wedding announcement was folded into the letter. The letter reads, in part:

> "My dearest beloved sister:
>
> It isn't without a great big sigh and a *bigger little* pain down in my heart that I begin this my last letter before the scene is changed. That might surprise my mother who claims to believe that I have no feelings, because I don't talk about them. I sometimes think that those who can speak of them don't always have the most sensitive ones. ...I am sure that you and Calvin are going to like one another very much. He is quiet and doesn't say much but what he does say amounts to something. That's one thing I like about him. ... These last weeks have been pretty hard for us all, I guess. Mother isn't very strong and she feels a little bit hard because I am going so hurriedly and sometimes she says things which strike in pretty deeply. She and Calvin set the time but she says he was very persistent. He talked with father later in the day and he called him very reasonable....Well, it is almost over, anyhow, and time will effect a cure, I think.
>
> With unending and unbounded love,
> Always your own devoted Sister"[21]

---

[18] Bittinger, "Calvin Coolidge's Courting Letters, 1904-1905," *The New England Journal of History*, p. 70.
[19] Gloria May Stoddard, *Grace and Cal: A Vermont Love Story* (Shelburne, Vermont: The New England Press, 1989) p. 12-13.
[20] Ross, p. 18.
[21] Grace Coolidge, Ivah Gale Collection.

Fortunately, other family members took a more positive view of the couple. Calvin had dated Grace in Northampton, but he took her to Plymouth, Vermont where he had grown up and she had met his relatives. Both Colonel John Coolidge, Calvin's father, and Carrie A. Brown Coolidge, his stepmother, approved of his choice. His grandmother, Sarah Almeda Brewer even suggested Calvin marry Grace before he mentioned the subject. Lemira's half sister, Mary Barrett, of Boston, was in favor. For the most part "the feeling prevailed, even in Northampton where Coolidge had a sound political rating, that he was the lucky one."[22]

The Goodhue family Bible, treasured by the Coolidge family, has a wedding announcement pasted inside. It begins, "A quiet home wedding occurred yesterday afternoon at 2:30 o'clock at the home of Mr. and Mrs. A. I. Goodhue, when their daughter, Miss Grace A. Goodhue, became the bride of Calvin Coolidge, an attorney of Northampton, Mass. The ceremony was performed by the Rev. Edward Hungerford in the presence of a small circle of relatives. There were no attendants. ...Among those present at the ceremony were Col. and Mrs. John C. Coolidge of Plymouth, parents of the groom, Mr. and Mrs. Don C. Pollard of Proctorsville, his aunt and uncle, and Miss Ethel Stevens, a class-mate of Miss Goodhue."[23]

The parlor at 312 Maple Street was quite small and was filled with good cheer and good will from 25 friends and relatives. However, Grace wrote of the day, "My mother was not in her usual good health, and the wedding was a quiet one, to which no formal invitations had been issued."[24] Fragrant clematis was arranged. Grace's dress was "pearl-gray silk etamine, made simply with a train"; Calvin wore a Prince Albert suit.[25] "The house was decorated for the event with evergreen and flowers festooned about the parlor..."[26] Grace enthusiastically sent a goodly number of announcements to family and friends. She was very excited. She could not remember the exact time their train was to depart after the wedding, but knew they were heading to Montreal for a week or so and then would then

---

[22] Ross, p. 19.
[23] John Coolidge private collection, The Goodhue Family Bible.
[24] *Grace Coolidge: An Autobiography*, p. 32.
[25] Ibid.
[26] Burlington Vermont newspaper clipping in Goodhue Bible.

return to "pack up, and start for Northampton" as a couple.[27] They were anxious to set up their first home, but for now they found temporary lodging at the Hotel Norwood while they scouted for a permanent residence.

---

[27] Grace Goodhue to Ivah Gale, October 1, 1905, Ivah Gale Collection.

Chapter 4

NORTHAMPTON YEARS

"Marriage is the most intricate institution set up by the human race. If it is to be a going concern it must have a head. That head should be the member of the firm who assumes the greater responsibility for its continuance. In general this is the husband....In my humble opinion the woman is by nature the more adaptable of the two and she should rejoice in this and realize that in the exercise of this ability she will obtain not only a spiritual blessing but her own family will rise up and call her blessed."[1]

Of course, Grace Coolidge wrote this after her marriage had progressed some 25 years, but this was her insight into her status. She was to be the supportive one. She was to raise children and keep home life running smoothly. She had stopped teaching and lost that meager income, so she was dependent on her husband's income and budgets. She had not taken her mother's advice to spend a year back in Burlington and her parents would not offer her financial support. She had a middle class life style with her husband's income as the source of funds. Her own desires and ambitions needed to be submerged for the sake of their joint operation. She wrote that her tightly budgeted lifestyle should not elicit pity. "What matter these trappings if love is strong and life is sweet?"[2] They even left their Montreal honeymoon early to set up housekeeping in Northampton and continue Calvin's political career.

The couple was fortunate because a professor was leaving town and wanted to rent his house completely furnished. In November of 1905 they moved in for the winter and even kept the maid on. That was added expense, but a big help to Grace since she had not really set up a kitchen before or learned to cook. She had

---

[1] *Grace Coolidge: An Autobiography*, p. 34-35.
[2] Ibid., p. 35.

been a teacher and eaten at the dining room at the residential school. In August of 1906 they moved to 21 Massasoit Street to occupy half of a two family house.

Grace was a happy wife devoted to her husband's success. As biographer Allison Lockwood observed, "The graceful, swinging stride of Grace Coolidge is unforgettable. She walked joyously, briskly, and at times seemed about to skip....She was one of those rare adults whose attentions delight rather than vaguely repel a child."[3] This was the end of a Victorian era so Grace dressed in high laced boots, long braided jackets and long skirts.[4]

Humor and teasing were a part of their lives from the early days of their marriage. Once they went to the grocery store and Grace asked her husband what Northampton people called kid-glove oranges. He said, "tautogs" full well knowing that was a variety of fish. When she asked for tautogs, the clerk gave a puzzled look. She was forced to point out with her hand what she wanted and was embarrassed.[5] Calvin also presented Grace 52 pairs of socks filled with holes to be darned when they first married. Grace kidded that he married her to get his socks darned![6] She also bought an expensive book entitled *Family Physician* full of medical information for eight dollars. Calvin, when she was not looking, wrote in the book, "Don't see any recipes for curing suckers."[7]

The two also began their long history as pet lovers. Bounder, a tiger kitten, was sent down to them from Calvin's father in Vermont and Climber soon followed. When a friend gave Grace a Maltese Angora cat, Calvin made fun of him by calling him "Mud."[8] As Grace once listed their first pets: Bounder and Climber as country cousins from Vermont, Mud, the unappreciated, and Judy, the timid.[9] Grace and Calvin enjoyed playing with their pets and found them a relaxing way to enjoy their life together.

Grace implied in her writings that her husband did not consider her as having "a serious turn of mind."[10] He was apt to discuss Plymouth and his boyhood with her, but "we seldom discussed current events, history, government, philosophy or religion."[11] She was to turn to her female friends for that kind of discussion. With

---

[3] Allison Lockwood, *A President in a Two Family House: Calvin Coolidge of Northampton* (Northampton: Northampton Historical Society, 1988) p. 3.
[4] Ross, p. 24.
[5] Ibid., p. 37.
[6] *The Real Calvin Coolidge #2*, p. 2.
[7] Stoddard., p. 16.
[8] Ibid., p. 16-17.
[9] Manuscript for *Good Housekeeping* articles, Forbes Library
[10] Ibid., Ms/9/1d
[11] Ibid.

her husband the main topics would be running the house, planning their social life, caring for their pets, caring for relatives and friends, and raising children.

Calvin had continually asked his father for financial support. With his new wife, he had "to keep running expenses low enough so that something may be saved to meet the day when earnings may be small."[12] The Coolidges shared a party phone line and used public transportation. Grace made her own dresses. They did very little entertaining or traveling. They were getting established. Calvin was known for his "probity, industry, thrift and reticence, for being 'on the job every day and all day.'" [13]He did lose one election soon after his marriage when he was defeated for School Committee. When he asked a neighbor why he did not vote for him, the man said that a school board member should have children in the public schools. Calvin's famous reply was, "Might give me some time!"[14] Calvin also believed that he was a politician who had served the party committee very well and was not the type for a local school board after all. He felt he "was better off attending to (his) law practice and (his) new home."[15] Grace concurred in these decisions.

Their move to 21 Massasoit Street was ideal with its intown location. The home was near the Clarke School for the Deaf and also near Smith College. It was less than two miles to the main street in Northampton and the electric trolley was being built. Electricity and a sewer system made this progressive town very desirable.

Renting half of a two family house and furnishing it was a rather hasty matter since Grace was pregnant with their first child during the spring and summer of 1906. Calvin bought furnishings such as an oak bedroom set, and installed his college bookcase. Grace's father, Captain Goodhue, had given them a couch. "The house was a simple frame dwelling, with three bedrooms and bath, a parlor, dining room, kitchen and attic. The front room had bay windows, where Grace sat with her knitting and sewing."[16] Their linens and silver came from a sale at the Norwood Hotel that was going out of business. Grace wrote, "that it is not necessary to have monogrammed linen of finest texture, nor solid silver marked in the latest script, in order to find happiness. I have much sentiment about those early possessions."[17]

---

[12] Fuess, p. 91.
[13] Ibid., p. 92
[14] Ibid., p. 90.
[15] *The Autobiography of Calvin Coolidge*, p. 94-95.
[16] Ross, p. 25.
[17] *Grace Coolidge: An Autobiography*, p. 35.

Ivah Gale, Grace's friend, saved the following letter from Calvin Coolidge dated September 10th, 1906, "Dear Ivah: Our boy came Friday at six p.m. Grace and he are perfectly well. She was sick only a short time. He has blue eyes and dark hair. He will be light like his Aunt Ivah. Grace and the boy send love. Yours Sincerely, Calvin Coolidge."[18] Coolidge was obviously excited. In his *Autobiography* written in 1929, he remembered the day with these words, "The fragrance of the clematis which covered the bay window filled the room like a benediction, where the mother lay with her baby. We called him John in honor of my father. It was all very wonderful to us."[19] Grace also wrote of the birth of their son, "This occurred at twilight on the seventh of September, as the whistles were blowing and the bells of the city clocks were striking the hour of six. The nurse and babe kept open house in the warm kitchen, a half hour later, while she was washing and dressing the infant, and I was told that our first-born appeared unusually appreciative of the attention for so young a child."[20]

Despite their excitement over this wonderful child, feeding the baby was not going that well. "The child had not thriven well during the first months of his life."[21] Grace's milk supply was "scanty" and a neighbor helped with a formula which helped her son grow. Grace's mother did not come to help her at this time so one would assume that the conflict with her mother was still somewhat of a problem. Calvin's family did not visit either but the new father proudly wrote to his own father, "Little John is as strong and smart as can be. He has blue eyes and red eyebrows. Grace calls his hair red. He weighed about 8 pounds and measures about 20 inches. They all say he looks just like me. His little hands are just like yours. I wish you could see him."[22] Grace was unsure about being left alone with her newborn son. Her husband had won a seat in the House of Representatives of the General Court in Massachusetts and would be in Boston most of the week. As a modern parent, she hoped she could share child rearing with her husband. He, in contrast, was brought up by his mother and at age two saw his father travel across the state as a representative to the state capital in Vermont, Montpelier. Grace wrote, "It was a new experience for me to assume so great responsibility for so precious a possession."[23] Luckily, she was in a town where she had lived since her college graduation and had made friends at the Clarke School for the Deaf and in

---

[18] Calvin Coolidge to Ivah Gale, Ivah Gale Collection.
[19] *The Autobiography of Calvin Coolidge*, p. 95.
[20] *Grace Coolidge: An Autobiography*, p. 39.
[21] Ibid, p. 40.
[22] Calvin Coolidge to his father, September 11, 1906 cited in Edward Connery Lathem, ed., *Your Son, Calvin Coolidge, A Selection of Letters from Calvin Coolidge to his Father* (Montpelier: Vermont Historical Society, 1968) p. 105.
[23] *Grace Coolidge: An Autobiography*, p. 40.

her neighborhood. This was the start of her life as a mother without the father being home every night as her father had been. The happy times Grace had with her own father were not to be repeated here with a father absent most of the week.

When he went to assume his seat in the General Court in Boston, Calvin took a rather strange letter to the Speaker of the House from a former State Senator, Dick Irwin of Northampton. "This will introduce you to the new member-elect from my town, Calvin Coolidge. Like the singed cat, he is better than he looks. He wishes to talk with you about committees. Anything you can do for him will be appreciated."[24] Calvin was to live in Spartan quarters at the Adams House near the State House in Boston. He commuted from Northampton by train, departing, Monday at 7:40 a.m. and returning, Friday at 7:25 p.m.; the new father was away during the week and home weekends. The family did travel home to Plymouth in the summer of 1907 and the proud father afterward wrote back to his father, "John creeps up on his knees now and goes up stairs and runs all over the house."[25] The big news was that Grace was expecting another baby who arrived in April of 1908. In the meantime, Calvin won a second term to the General Court.

Grace was determined to name their second son after Calvin but he resisted this tradition for some time so they called the baby "Bun" for bunny for a few days. He looked a lot like the mother Calvin had lost at age twelve and "an unusually strong bond" developed between him and this son.[26]

Grace saw that her husband had to give most of his time to his work, but determined that she would try to replicate her childhood by giving as much time and as many opportunities as she could to the boys. She was a "stay at home" mother and as she wrote, "I gave my entire time to it, and I know of no investment which yields such large and satisfactory returns."[27]

Calvin Jr. became ill at age five and had an operation for emphysema and both parents were very concerned. "Calvin has been sick a week this noon with pneumonia. It is in his lower right lung. He does not seem to be suffering much now from pain but has fever running from 99 to 103 (sic) it is 100 this morning the nurse says. We think he is better, unless it gets into his other lung we think he will get well but he is very sick still. He has a strong constitution and fights disease and his heart action is good."[28] The father continued in another letter, "He is very thin and weak, but you would be proud to see how much courage he has.

---

[24] Fuess, p. 96.
[25] Ibid., p. 101.
[26] *Grace Coolidge: An Autobiography*, p. 40.
[27] Ibid., p. 41.
[28] *Your Son, Calvin Coolidge*, p. 123-124. (English errors by Calvin Coolidge.)

He is a thoroughbred."[29] Grace spent all her time in the hospital watching over his surgery and his fitting with a drainage tube. With a tube in his back for further drainage, Calvin Jr. returned home accompanied by a nurse to assist him. Thankfully he did recover, the tube was removed, and he returned to a regular boy's life. This scare brought the parents together and made father Calvin bond even more to his fragile son.

Grace created activities for the boys and encouraged their sports. John "had a natural ability in handling tools" and was the social one.[30] Since John and his mother built a roadster, he was a bit surprised when he saw a newspaper photograph of his father, when running for office, posing with son Calvin, as if they had built the automobile he built during a summer vacation with his mother![31] His brother was more of a book worm with an ability to see "straight to the heart of a matter, of thinking through to a conclusion,…and to answer to a question in the fewest possible words."[32] He was also a tease like his father. The neighborhood boys were their friends. Jack Hills, one of them, was the son of Mr. and Mrs. R.B. Hills; his mother, Teresa, was to become a lifelong friend of Grace's. Music was important to the family with Grace playing the piano while John played the violin and Calvin Jr. played a banjo-mandolin. They enjoyed singing church hymns at Edwards Church in central Northampton. Grace was very proud that she joined the church when she first arrived in town and now both boys were regular church goers. She hoped that her strong religious beliefs which grounded and comforted her would also be their guide.

Grace later wrote that her husband, in these early years of married life, liked to take the family to Rahar's Inn for a Sunday night supper. The first time there, little Calvin asked what to do about the finger bowls with lemons. His father suggested he drink from the bowl and this he did.[33] Once again, Calvin, the father, was enjoying his pranks and teasing. Both boys, when old enough, had paper routes and their earnings were deposited at the local savings bank. One day they were walking with their father and passed the bank and (as son John wrote) he "stopped and told us to listen. There seemed to be nothing unusual to listen to, and doubtless our facial expressions gave clear evidence that we were puzzled. After an interval of silence, with our attention fixed for his next remark, he asked, "Can you hear your money working for you?"[34]

---

[29] Ibid., p. 124.
[30] Ibid., p. 46.
[31] Ibid, p. 33.
[32] Interview with John Coolidge, summer of 1999 and ibid, p. 40.
[33] *The Real Calvin Coolidge #1*, p. 27.
[34] *The Real Calvin Coolidge # 9*, p. 32.

Grace provided some balance since her husband was quite stern with the boys. He reproved them sharply and "was impatient" with their shortcomings since "life was a serious matter with him."[35] She wrote, "He required and received prompt obedience. Yet he ruled by direction and precept rather than by force."[36] As for the teasing, Calvin Jr. often outwitted his father. John "was a more shy and sensitive child" and must have fallen many times for his father's wit.[37] Since father Calvin did not spend much time with the boys due to his busy career, they probably did not get the benefit of the positive side of his nature as much as they might have wished. When Calvin Jr. received a 50 in deportment at school, Grace was the one to visit the teacher and institute the punishment of no reading after dinner and no skis for Christmas. The teacher remembered Grace as a "vivid, buoyant mother and friend."[38] The boys were to do their homework, clean the dishes, mow the grass, and be frank and truthful. Grace set up a tent in the backyard and even built a playhouse out of recycled materials. She was the one to play baseball and board games with them.[39] She enjoyed play and sports and was happy to spend time with her boys in this way. Her husband was too serious and too busy to do this.

The head of the household's political career had to take precedence over everything else. In 1906 and 1907, Calvin commuted to Boston to serve as Northampton's representative to the General Court and joined 240 men, of whom four were from Hampshire County. A salary of $750 a year was not large, but the session from January to June allowed him to do other legal work at home. Serving in the General Court was "almost essential for a fledging statesman seeking advancement in politics in Massachusetts."[40] Calvin lived very simply in Boston at the Adams House, occupying only a small room without a bath and with only a washbowl. He could cross the street to visit the Western Massachusetts Club for larger space to read the paper, converse with colleagues and have a pot of green tea. In 1908, he did not run, preferring to return to his law practice, but his party urged him to run for mayor of Northampton as "the man to bring the city government back to the Republican Party."[41]

In 1909, he was duly elected mayor and re-elected in 1910 so he had two years at home with the family. He had turned down the increased salary voted in that year as a gesture to uphold a tight budget for the town. However, he was once

---

[35] Ibid.
[36] Ibid., p. 34.
[37] Ibid.
[38] Ross, p. 38
[39] Ibid., p..39.
[40] Fuess, p. 95.

again strapped for funds and asked his father for assistance. He wrote him, "Grace has got to have a suit, a dress, an evening dress, an evening wrap, and a dress hat and street hat, total about $300 or more."[42] He was conscious of his own clothes and that of his wife. He wanted to be proud of her appearance. Calvin's own father became a Vermont State Senator, so he was very proud of his family and noted that son John, only age four, "is worthy to bear your name."[43]

Grace was the "safety valve" for her husband. As he became annoyed with any obstacles in his path, she heard the "explosions."[44] He felt that being a mayor was expensive and "takes much time."[45] He did not have the patience for it. Grace took the opportunity to attend musical events with the free tickets a mayor received from the Academy of Music and she was pleased with his time at home. He saw a political opening and ran for state senator to represent 17 towns in 1911 and was re-elected each November until he ran for lieutenant-governor in 1915. He found the new work load heavy with 2000 bills to consider in one session, but he was accumulating power in the Senate.[46] His reasoning and judgment were becoming more respected by his colleagues and he was gaining statewide recognition.

Meanwhile, Calvin and Grace Coolidge had formed a family life in Northampton; Grace also created a social life and a life of community involvement. She began the Children's Home Association with a temporary shelter on Arlington Street. "This facility served as a temporary home until foster family homes could be located for waiting children."[47] She was involved in the good works of Edwards Church and sewed items for their bazaars. She went to market with Mrs. Reuben B. Hills and would go with her to Boston to listen to her husband's political speeches. She spent time with Mrs. Florence B. Adams, another neighbor, whose daughter Janey was fond of the Coolidge family. Since Calvin was away so much, Grace developed her own network of friends. Already recognizing that she would like some activities with adults that did not include their children, Calvin watched the boys on some Saturday nights so she could go out with friends.[48] He was trying to accommodate her interests. Their social life together centered around the young couples of the town who attended dance parties at different homes where Grace wanted to learn all the new steps. Calvin

---

[41] Ibid., p. 104.
[42] Ibid., p. 105.
[43] Ibid., p. 108.
[44] *The Real Calvin Coolidge #2*, p. 13.
[45] Fuess, p. 109.
[46] Ibid., p. 112.
[47] "Agency Profile" Children's Aid and Family Service of Hampshire County archive.
[48] Ross, p. 35.

did not dance, he watched. They did play croquet together in summer and participated in outdoor roasts. Grace was curious about the world outside of New England. She even volunteered to chaperone a group of seniors from Northampton High School on a tour of Washington, D.C. in 1912 to take in the sights.

Calvin and Grace Coolidge on the telephone, 1915 (The Calvin Coolidge Memorial Foundation (CCMF) archives)

Another part of Grace's social life and life of contribution was her devotion to the Pi Beta Phi's. She offered 21 Massasoit Street as a "regular meeting place for the Pi Phi's and in 1910 she became president of the recently organized Western Massachusetts Pi Beta Phi Alumnae Club."[49] The gatherings were social in nature

---

[49] Becque, p. 12.

with thimble parties, lunches, and picnics drawing women from nine chapters in eleven towns. She was voted in as Vice President of Alpha Province, an area from Toronto to Florida, at the 1912 convention in Illinois. One of the goals of her fraternity was to create the Settlement School of Gatlinburg, Tennessee which opened in that year to educate children as well as provide a way to sell native handicrafts.

Grace must have realized that her husband was slated for a higher office when he became president of the Massachusetts Senate on January 7, 1914. She was in the gallery when he gave his famous inaugural speech upon assuming that position, "Have Faith in Massachusetts." She saw the positive reaction to his words. She comprehended that men were willing to follow him as a leader in his party. His advice that day, in part, was as follows:

> "Do the day's work. If it be to protect the rights of the weak, whoever objects, do it. If it be to help a powerful corporation better to serve the people, whatever the opposition, do that. Expect to be called a stand-patter, but don't be a stand-patter. Expect to be called a demagogue, but don't be a demagogue. Don't hesitate to be as revolutionary as science. Don't hesitate to be as reactionary as the multiplication table. Don't expect to build up the weak by pulling down the strong. Don't hurry to legislate. Give administration a chance to catch up with legislation."[50]

Calvin also expressed his opinion that mankind primarily responds to things of the spirit and that "all men are peers."

The legislator, Calvin Coolidge, made a point of studying his subjects more than anyone else he knew. The *Springfield Republican*, a local Hampshire County newspaper, commented on State Senator Coolidge, "He is one of the most cautious men in the Senate, and he is one of the most quiet."[51] He "impressed others by his knowledge, his parliamentary skill, his quiet patience, and his sagacity....He had few enemies and many loyal friends."[52] Grace could see that her husband was gaining support in the press and among his colleagues.

Actually Calvin's speeches were part of his political success. He wrote them at home or in his Boston quarters on yellow foolscap and then dictated them to his secretary. Grace "never disturbed him when he was preparing a speech, nor did (she) know what was going into it."[53] Coolidge felt these speeches were his

---

[50] Coolidge, *Have Faith in Massachusetts* (Boston: Houghton Mifflin, 1919) p.7-8.
[51] Fuess, p. 113.
[52] Ibid.
[53] Ross, p. 46.

"works of art" and that "every word in them had to be considered much of a strain to do over again."[54]

Grace Coolidge was present during the event that was the turning point of her husband's career. Frank Waterman Stearns, an Amherst graduate in the class of 1878, arranged a dinner in honor of her husband for Amherst graduates and faculty. This dinner at the Algonquin Club in Boston was scheduled for May 12, 1915 with 65 in attendance, and a goal by the Amherst men of considering Calvin Coolidge for the office of Lieutenant Governor. Stearns sent Grace Coolidge flowers after the dinner and Calvin wrote, "I think the experience has revealed to me in a new light the meaning of Amherst College."[55] Calvin also thanked Mrs. Stearns for "engrossing" the invitation and making the place cards.[56] This began a lifetime association for both the couples. Stearns was a "merchant of high character...but entirely without experience in politics."[57] Mrs. Stearns was a Williston, a member of a well known family in Western Massachusetts. She was well connected and also willing to extend herself to introduce Grace to people of influence in the state.

Frank Stearns chose to support and encourage Calvin Coolidge. At times, Calvin was not so sure he would succeed in the political world. He wrote to Stearns in June of 1915, "I am a little embarrassed to have you doing so much without knowing that I can ever supplement your efforts and think I ought to warn you that your energy may be thrown away so far as any political developments are concerned."[58]

Despite Calvin's misgivings, the couple had arrived in Boston's society and in Boston's politics. The Amherst connection made all the difference. The May 12th dinner was held at the Algonquin Club, designed in the Italian Renaissance Palazzo style by McKim, Meade and White in 1888, and a prominent landmark on Commonwealth Avenue. Art and sculpture adorned the rooms and the main dining room had four fireplaces.[59] Grace and her husband were now to be part of a plan to advance an "Amherst man." Calvin, however, encouraged his wife to leave town as planned with her fraternity since he said he would follow her to the West Coast on July 18. Calvin then conferred with Northampton politicians and

---

[54] Edward Connery Lathem,ed., *Meet Calvin Coolidge* (Brattleboro, Vermont: The Stephen Greene Press, 1960), p. 130.
[55] Letter from Calvin Coolidge to Frank W. Stearns, May 13, 1915, Stearns Collection, Amherst College Archives and Special Collections, Amherst College Library, Amherst, Massachusetts.
[56] Letter from Calvin Coolidge to Frank W. Stearns, May 18, 1915, Stearns Collection.
[57] *The Autobiography of Calvin Coolidge*, p. 113.
[58] Calvin Coolidge letter to Frank W. Stearns, June 3, 1915, Stearns Collection.
[59] The Algonguin Club of Boston website

Stearns back at the Algonquin Club and declared himself a candidate for Lieutenant Governor and stayed in Massachusetts.

Grace crossed the country with her fraternity sisters traveling in cars, buses, and trains. The New England delegates partied all the way out. "We sang and sang, and when we ran out of songs we all knew, some sang chapter songs."[60] When they reached San Francisco, the Boston group toured the Pan-American Exposition and other local sites. Grace was elected Alpha Province president at the convention but was called home to help her husband run for office. She did not return with the delegates, but immediately set out to help her husband become Lt. Governor of their state of Massachusetts. She had had fun, but saw that life was to get more serious for her and her family. A statewide office was more pressure and would entail more of a contribution from her. She was needed back home.

Before Grace left California, the Massachusetts and Vermont fraternity delegates decided to create a Round Robin set of letters. One person started the round by writing a letter, each new person added her letter until 14 were in the pack, then on the round began again and each person replaced her letter with a new one. Grace wrote her sisters the rest of her life in these robins. She offered her opinions and discussed books and events that impressed her in these letters. They were a place where she could express herself and her opinions would be kept confidential. She enjoyed the freedom of exchange.

Back in Massachusetts, the campaign for Lt. Governor widened the political and social life of the couple. Frank Stearns offered to pay the candidate's expenses. He knew that Calvin did not have the resources to even consider this. Publicity had to be generated and the usual posters and stationary needed to be printed. Besides the costs of the political campaign, Stearns worried about the impact on the Coolidge family's resources and he offered to give them funding. Calvin Coolidge wrote Stearns on his State House stationary, "I have everything we need and am able to save something. I do not think a man who cannot take care of himself is worthy of very much consideration."[61] Coolidge was rather a reluctant candidate. Once it was decided he was going to run, an executive committee was formed with Stearns as chairman and Calvin planned to write all the state committees and chairmen of cities and towns and legislators. Frank W. Stearns wrote newspapers and other influential friends that Coolidge had experience and a fine public record. Coolidge's colleagues in the General Court

---

[60] Ibid., p. 16.
[61] Calvin Coolidge letter to Frank W. Stearns, undated, Stearns Collection.

respected him and were "controlling figures in their respective districts."[62] Calvin's letter to Stearns from Burlington, Vermont showed that a visit to Grace's family did not keep the candidate from attending to his campaign.

Stearns raised funds and promoted his man everywhere noting that "he must be Governor and still later President."[63] Calvin appreciated the work Stearns did for him and wrote to him, "I should not have been where I am had it not been for you."[64] Now the future political success of the Coolidges would be entwined with the campaign abilities of Frank Stearns. The two couples were beginning to spend more time together as this enterprise got going. Coolidge spoke from cars during the day and in halls in the evening as he toured the state sometimes making 15 speeches a day. All of this without the "graces of oratory," according to his mentor Stearns.[65] In 1916, the Republicans had won control of the Executive and both branches of the General Court in Massachusetts, the first time since 1909. As Lt. Governor, Calvin reviewed state expenses, analyzed the details of administration and visited institutions throughout the state.

Calvin's success meant that he would primarily be in Boston and Grace would continue to raise the boys in Northampton. She would need to travel between both areas to appear with Calvin at special events. She also decided to turn down the Province presidency of the Pi Beta Phi fraternity, not just on Calvin's account but also due to concern about the health and well being of her mother.[66]

In April 1917, the United States entered World War I, bringing profound and lasting changes to the nation. "The response which the people made and the organizing power of the country were all manifestations that it was wonderful to contemplate. The entire nation awoke to a new life," wrote Calvin Coolidge.[67] In Northampton, now a town of 21,500, a minor building boom was expanding the town beyond its borders. Nearby Amherst College was filled with men preparing for military service.[68] After Calvin Coolidge's mayoralty of frugal administration, the city raised salaries for personnel and built a new high school after a fire took

---

[62] Fuess, p. 139.
[63] Fuess, p. 137.
[64] Fuess, p. 141.
[65] Fuess, p. 147.
[66] Letter to Pi Beta Phi Fraternity from Grace Coolidge, Sept. 8, 1915, Pi Beta Phi Archives, Pi Beta Phi Fraternity, Town and Country, Missouri.
[67] *The Autobiography of Calvin Coolidge*, p. 121.
[68] Fuess, Claude M. *Amherst, The Story of a New England College* (Boston: Little, Brown, and Co., 1935) p. 316.

the old one. Calvin would occasionally be back in town to give a speech.[69] He served three terms as Lt. Governor and kept his law office open in Northampton but did not turn any government business over to it. Grace still kept a tight budget since her husband's salary was only $2,000 a year.

Calvin and Grace Coolidge, John and Calvin Jr., 1916 (Courtesy Vermont Historical Society, Barre; Coolidge Family Photos, Doc.221)

"It was no secret that I desired to be Governor," wrote Coolidge.[70] Grace began preparing for the eventuality. Even though she stayed in the background, Frank Stearns knew her importance and wrote, "Of course many others can claim

---

[69] The Tercentenary History Committee, *The Northampton Book* (Brattleboro, Vermont:Alan S. Browne, Inc., 1954) p. 312.
[70] *The Autobiography of Calvin Coolidge*, p. 121.

to have picked him out, but amongst them all I think we can shake hands over the proposition that yours was the most important endorsement and mine comes next."[71] While Coolidge was Lt. Governor, Grace joined Mrs. Stearns to hear her husband speak at the Copley Plaza Hotel on February 4, 1916, in Boston for the Amherst College Alumni Association. She rarely heard her husband speak in public and did not really know how "rasping" his Vermont Yankee pronunciation was.[72] She hid her laughter behind a pillar when her husband's nasal twang rang out on a quotation![73] She could see that he "was not magnetic," could not "sway great audiences" with his powers of speech, but "the people who heard him remembered who he was and talked over what he had said."[74] The Stearnses took the Coolidges to New York and Washington D.C. to stay at the luxurious Shoreham Hotel. They were being courted as a couple to join the political circles. The Stearnses felt that they could make their life more comfortable. They were entertained by the patrician Henry Cabot Lodge, the Senator from Massachusetts, even though he had acted superior to the Coolidges, such a middle class couple.

Grace could see that her husband's promotion of "the right of the people to be well born, well reared, well educated, well employed and well paid" combined with his fiscal austerity had great appeal.[75] Calvin was detained in Boston many days due to war emergencies and rarely even returned home on weekends.[76] He helped form a Public Safety Committee and urged the equipping of state troops. When Governor McCall decided not to run again after three terms, he suggested Coolidge declare his candidacy for the office. Calvin was nominated by his party without opposition. The campaign was "difficult" but the *Boston Herald* newspaper declared Coolidge a constructionist and his opponent, Long, a profiteer.[77]

After his election to the governorship, Grace and Calvin did travel to Maine for a conference but returned after the signing of the Armistice ending World War I to be in Boston for November 12th, Victory Day. "Never has a Massachusetts man been better qualified by experience and training for the Governorship than Calvin Coolidge," wrote biographer Fuess.[78] Northampton citizens decided to fete their newly acclaimed couple. When, on November 15, 1918, Calvin and Grace took the train back from Boston, they were met by "a cheering crowd" and a

---

[71] Fuess, *The Man from Vermont, Calvin Coolidge*, p. 145
[72] Ibid., p. 153.
[73] Ibid., p. 153.
[74] Ibid., p. 154.
[75] Ibid., p. 175.
[76] Ibid., p. 167.
[77] Ibid., p. 169.
[78] Ibid., p. 171.

parade was formed to accompany them with a band. They were cheered when they attended the Northampton Players performance as a family that evening. Col. John Coolidge, father of the new governor, came down for the swearing in ceremony in Boston in January of 1919 and Grace triumphantly led the grand march at the inaugural ball. The new first lady of Massachusetts took great joy in the elevation of her husband to the highest office in the state.

Massachusetts did not have an executive mansion. Now that he was governor, Calvin rented an extra room at Adams House and Grace stayed behind in Northampton with the boys. "She had never taken any part in my political life, but had given her attention to our home."[79] Frank Stearns and his wife changed this with their invitations and plans to hold lunches for Mrs. Coolidge with a "carefully selected list of ladies."[80] Stearns was the first one to see her political value. "One of his greatest assets is Mrs. Coolidge. She will make friends wherever she goes, and she will not meddle with his conduct of the office."[81] Stearns went so far as to propose the family move to Beacon Hill and get adequate help so Mrs. Coolidge could "entertain constantly."[82] "The whole scheme is to get him actually known to every citizen in Massachusetts and some from outside."[83] Calvin, without hesitation, turned down the offer. However, he did enjoy his new ornate office space with its black and gold Italian mantel and two tall windows in the southwest corner of the third floor of the old Bulfinch State House.[84] He often lunched at the Union Club, but he did not become part of the inner circle of Boston's elite as Stearns had hoped he would, nor did Grace move to Boston with the boys. However, she was treated differently now that she was widely recognized as wife of the governor. When attending a Smith College program, she was seated with the faculty wives. In Northampton, she had arrived!

---

[79] Ibid.
[80] Ibid., p. 177.
[81] Ibid.
[82] Ibid., p. 178.
[83] Ibid.
[84] Ibid., p. 181.

Chapter 5

HEADING TO THE NATIONAL STAGE

"After reading all the good letters, I am left speechless—or writeless—by all the nice things you have said in regard to a certain member of my family. I am wondering if this Robin wouldn't make a good campaign literature. It might be headed, 'We are advertised by our loving friends.'"[1]

Grace was almost breathless in this correspondence with her round robin fraternity sisters. Her husband, Governor Calvin Coolidge, had become famous nationally with his handling of the Boston Police Strike of 1919. Before the strike he sympathized with the police's drive to form a union by stating, "Can you blame the police for feeling as they do when they get less than a street-car conductor?"[2] The policemen knew that they were not allowed to form a union, but they started to do so and when the Police Commissioner overruled them, Governor Coolidge backed him. As a result, Coolidge expected his own "defeat in the coming campaign for re-election as Governor."[3] Three quarters of the police force left their duties and soon after midnight, September 9th, rioting and disorder broke out. The Mayor called out the State Guard within Boston and requested the Governor furnish more troops. Coolidge called out the entire State Guard and order was quickly restored in the city of Boston.[4] President Wilson declared the strike to be a "crime against civilization" and the press praised the governor's actions.[5]

Samuel Gompers, head of the national American Federation of Laborers, telegraphed the governor with a request to remove the police commissioner and

---

[1] Correspondence in the Round Robin Files, November 11, 1920, Pi Beta Phi Fraternity Archives.
[2] Lockwood, p. 7.
[3] *The Autobiography of Calvin Coolidge*, p. 128.
[4] Ibid., p. 131.

reinstate the union policemen. The governor telegraphed back, "There is no right to strike against the public safety by any body, any time, any where."[6] This statement caught the public's imagination and there was much comment on it and on Coolidge in the nation's press. As Calvin saw the issue, "if voluntary associations...be permitted to substitute their will for the authority of public officials the end of our government was at hand. The issue was nothing less than whether the law which the people had made through their duly authorized agencies should be supreme."[7] Calvin was pleased at his own "clearness of thought" and the power to perform his duty was somehow given to him, as he wrote his father.[8] Calvin thought his decision in the Boston Police Strike was more important than his own re-election. "The result wont [sic] matter to me but it will matter a great deal to all the rest of America."[9] Reading favorable cartoons and laudatory editorials about her husband, Grace now had no doubt that her husband had become famous. She would be called upon to travel more and make plans to have others supervise the boys in her absence.

The Republican state convention in October of 1919 was a high point in the Massachusetts career of Calvin Coolidge and a time where his wife was in the spotlight as well. Despite a bout with acute bronchitis, he appeared with Grace, their two sons, and his father, Col. John Coolidge, who attended with a "prominent place on the platform."[10] The delegates jumped to their feet in praise of their governor and in favor of his re-nomination. Three colleges quickly presented the governor their honorary degrees. Grace beamed as Calvin received LL.D. degrees from Amherst, Tufts, and Williams Colleges.[11] Calvin calmly ordered cheese from his father's factory in Plymouth and commented that prominent Democrats were supporting his ticket since his opponent disagreed with his handling of the Boston Police Strike.

In November of 1919, Coolidge won re-election as governor with an overwhelming vote, receiving the second largest plurality in the state's history. *The Boston Herald* hailed Coolidge's victory which "brought from all sections of the country messages of congratulation and joy that Massachusetts had stood firm against the forces of disorder and destruction. The contest here was watched by leading men all over the United States, and by them regarded as transcending in importance any election that has been held anywhere in the United States within

---

[5] Fuess, p. 223.
[6] Ibid., p. 134.
[7] Ibid.
[8] Ibid., p. 135.
[9] *Your Son, Calvin Coolidge*, letter to his father, September 26, 1919, p. 150.
[10] Ibid., October 10, 1919, p. 152.

the last decade, not excepting even Presidential elections."[12] President Wilson wired Coolidge, "I congratulate you upon your election as a victory for law and order. When that is the issue all Americans stand together."[13] Grace, at Adams House in Boston, where she was spending more time, wrote, after the election outcome, "It certainly was a great victory for law and order and no doubt the effect of it will be felt outside the boundaries of our own state."[14] She was hinting that there would be talk of national office and she knew that would mean more of her involvement.

Grace had a divided life now. She raised the boys in a middle class way in Northampton as her husband "moved up" in political circles and spent time in wealthy homes and hotels.[15] She and her husband tried to keep a strong family life despite the time she must now spend in Boston at special events without the boys. Even in the midst of the Boston Police strike, Calvin found time to return home for his son's birthday. Calvin wrote John that he must take life seriously now since he would be 13 years old, "It will only be a little while before you are a man."[16] "Being a good man is so important," he wrote, and "be good to your mother, since you are her first baby."[17]

Calvin's victory brought him into contention as a Presidential candidate for the Republican Party. The political focus at the time centered on Woodrow Wilson's campaign for the League of Nations which had ended in defeat on November 19, 1919, when the Senate rejected the Treaty of Versailles. The debate was about America's proper role in the world. With Theodore Roosevelt's death in January of 1919, there was no one dominant individual seeking the Republican presidential nomination. Rather, several candidates had emerged, including, along with Coolidge, General Leonard Wood, Governor Frank O. Lowden of Illinois, and Senator Warren G. Harding of Ohio. Coolidge's candidacy was being pushed by his friends in Massachusetts. He ignored it, tending instead to his duties as governor.

Calvin learned about his step-mother's health and took time out from politics to go with Grace and the boys to visit her and his father in Plymouth, Vermont in April of 1920. He was very dedicated to her since she had loved him so much and

---

[11] Ibid., p. 154.
[12] Ibid., p. 155.
[13] Fuess, p. 238-239.
[14] Correspondence of Grace Coolidge to Gene, November 6, 1919,(Imogene Prindle, a neighbor) Forbes Library Collection.
[15] Fuess, p. 201.
[16] Correspondence to son John, Coolidge Family Papers, Vermont Historical Society.
[17] Ibid.

encouraged him in all his political efforts. Her loss a few weeks later was a terrible blow to him. The family returned to Plymouth for her funeral on May 23rd.

Calvin urged his father to travel to Massachusetts so they could follow the Chicago Republican convention together, but the older man refused. Evidently some candidates were attempting to "buy" delegates. Governor Coolidge's campaign "has been conducted on a high plane and his candidacy has made an attractive picture to Republican voters generally."[18] Calvin did not campaign in the primaries. He did not feel that as governor he should be campaigning for higher office. However, his political friends were hard at work. Frank Stearns had relinquished management of his store to his subordinates, moved into the Back Bay in Boston, and arranged lunches and dinners for Calvin Coolidge to "meet the right people."[19] Drawing upon Coolidge's fame from the Police Strike, he printed up the governor's speeches in a book entitled *Have Faith in Massachusetts* and distributed 65,000 copies of it along with hundreds of photographs of the governor, framed and signed, to potential supporters. Stearns also opened campaign headquarters in Washington and Chicago and went to Chicago to campaign for Coolidge himself. In June, at the time of the convention, he provided each delegate with a pamphlet of Coolidge speeches entitled *Law and Order*. When the balloting began, Coolidge received thirty-four votes on the first ballot, but Warren G. Harding, with the backing of powerful Senators, was the eventual victor. "...Federal office holders who were bent on having one of their own" selected him, wrote Coolidge to his father.[20] Grace watched all this as they both relied on Frank Stearns to do his best to promote his man, Calvin Coolidge.

Grace Coolidge was in the room in Boston this time when her husband made the decision that would bring him so close to the presidency, a heart beat away actually. She was in Boston more now, staying at the Adams House with her husband or with the Stearnses at the Hotel Touraine. She was at Adams House when Calvin got the call that the Republican convention had nominated him for the vice presidency. Judge Wallace McCamant of Oregon, after Harding was deemed the duly chosen presidential candidate, dared to nominate Calvin Coolidge even though the convention bosses had already settled upon another individual. Coolidge was known and popular among the rank and file delegates because of his handling of the Police Strike and many of them had also read *Have Faith in Massachusetts*. The delegates rebelled against the bosses and nominated

---

[18] *Your Son, Calvin Coolidge*, p. 161.
[19] Francis Russell, *The President Makers, From Mark Hanna to Joseph P. Kennedy* (Boston: Little, Brown and Co, 1976), p. 252.
[20] *Your Son, Calvin Coolidge*, p. 166.

Coolidge giving a roar of approval. "He was overwhelmingly nominated."[21] "Nominated for Vice President!" Calvin told his wife after receiving a phone call from the convention. "You're not going to accept it, are you?" He replied, "I suppose I shall have to."[22] She probably agreed with Stearns who had seen the vice-presidency as a "dead-end post."[23] Calvin later wrote that in his quest for the presidency, he had just wanted to satisfy his father, Stearns, and Murray Crane, a former governor and mentor, but he accepted the vice presidential nomination and hoped his father would not mind.[24] The vice presidency, at this time, was not an exciting prospect. Shortly after the phone call, reporters stampeded into their rooms at Adams House and Calvin receded to a private room to write up a statement that he would accept the decision of the convention. The couple did not call their sons that day in Northampton but someone called their family physician and his boys raced up the street to tell John and Calvin Jr..[25]

Grace had lived for fifteen years with this unusual man, this new candidate for national office. She knew his private side -- his long silences and irritability. He was troubled with asthma and indigestion.[26] He did not suffer stuffed shirts or primadonnas very well. On the other hand, publicly, he was a perfect role model. His secretary, Henry F. Long, characterized him "as the kindest, most understanding man he ever met, deeply considerate of everyone around him."[27] Coolidge did not put on airs and made sure even his bodyguard obeyed the law. He said, "I am the first person in Massachusetts to obey the law, not the last."[28] He took the streetcar to events to avoid fanfare and be a man of the people. During the summer of 1920, they returned to Plymouth Notch for his July 4th birthday and relatives and friends came in to congratulate the nominee, this ideal candidate. On one day, 2,000 Vermonters came to greet him in Plymouth.

One of the happiest pictures of the Coolidge family of Northampton was taken of them in front of their house at 21 Massasoit Street on July 27, 1920, the day Governor Coolidge was notified by the leaders of the Republican Party at an impressive ceremony of his nomination for Vice President. Each member of the family looked handsome and well dressed. The boys were still in short pants, the fashion of the day. Grace was wearing a hat with a large brim. Their ages were Calvin, 48, Grace, 41, John, 13, and Calvin Jr. 12. The boys were old enough to

---

[21] Russell, p. 263.
[22] Lockwood, p. 8.
[23] Russell, p. 263.
[24] *Your Son, Calvin Coolidge*, p. 166.
[25] Lockwood, p. 8.
[26] Fuess, p. 197.
[27] Ibid., p. 198.
[28] Ibid., p. 199.

be proud of their father and this pride showed through in the photograph. The family knew the President of Smith College, L. Clark Seelye, who presided over the ceremony, and great things were expected from this favorite son. Grace realized they would return to Boston for his final work as governor. Now she was part of the team. However, when Calvin was sent to speak in the South she was to "keep the homefires burning" in Northampton and take care of a new pet.[29] She and Calvin wanted to give a Belgian police dog to his father, but when he refused to take the dog, the pet lovers, Calvin and Grace, kept him. Calvin wrote his father, "Your dog is growing well. She has bitten the ice man, the milkman, and the grocerman. It is good to have some way to get even with them for the high prices they charge for everything."[30]

A rally for Calvin in Boston on November 1, 1920, brought the campaign to a close. The Tremont Temple was overflowing as he spoke and then his state limousine whisked the couple home to Northampton so they could both vote. This was the first year that women could vote in federal elections and Grace proudly cast her ballot for the Harding-Coolidge ticket. Then they were driven back to Boston for they were to be guests of the Stearnses at the Hotel Touraine while the returns rolled in via telegraph and telephone. A huge blackboard in the hotel displayed the names of the states, their electoral votes, and the 1916 vote for comparison. Calvin was received with cheers at the American House, the City Club, and the Algonquin Club. Governor and Mrs. Coolidge celebrated a great victory on election day. The tallies: Harding/Coolidge ticket: 16,143,407; James M. Cox and Franklin D. Roosevelt: 9,130,328. Electoral votes: 404 Republican, 127 Democratic.

Since there was considerable time before the inauguration in March, Calvin continued to be heavily engaged at a governors' conference and various speaking engagements. The boys did participate in Calvin's last day as governor, but the various offers of vacations from Mr. and Mrs. Stearns were turned down with a few exceptions. Grace was still not getting much national exposure or training for her role in Washington. A trip to Asheville, North Carolina with Mr. and Mrs. Stearns was accepted. Stearns again complimented Grace by congratulating Calvin on choosing her "to be your helper in the work for others that you have done and are destined to do."[31] They traveled to Marion, Ohio to meet with Mr. and Mrs. Harding and plan for transition.

---

[29] Round Robin letter, Grace to Pi Beta Phi sisters, November 11, 1920, Pi Beta Phi Archives.
[30] *Your Son, Calvin Coolidge*, letter of November 1, 1920, p. 171.
[31] Fuess, p. 279.

The March 4, 1921 inauguration included a gathering of the Coolidges' small coterie: Col. John Coolidge, their sons, Mr. and Mrs. Stearns, and Mayor Fitzgerald of Northampton. The lunch at the White House was the first time the Coolidges were ever entertained there. They went to a dinner and ball at the Edward B. McLean's where Grace's dinner companion was General Pershing, a military hero. He, afterward, declared he was "won by her."[32] She was off to a good start. Since the couple was new to Washington they were being evaluated all the time. Grace was just now being introduced to the strain of public life.

The business of setting up a home and office in Washington was now a priority. Calvin was paid $12,000 a year and provided with a car and chauffeur. He had a secretary, page, clerk and telegraph operator. He had two offices, one at the Capitol and another in the Senate Office Building.[33]

Mrs. Coolidge resigned herself to hotel life since they turned down Mr. Stearns's offer of a home and the Vice President had no residence in those days. With a salary of $12,000 a year, maintaining a house would have been quite a task. They were to live in Suite 328 with two bedrooms, a dining room, and large reception room in the New Willard Hotel.[34] The boys had been left behind in Massachusetts until a boarding school could be arranged for them in the fall. When Grace left the capital to check on their children, Calvin was lonely. He wrote his father, "Grace is home as you may know from the papers. She is wonderfully popular here. I don't know what I would do without her."[35] He was becoming very dependent on his talkative wife who could quickly engage people and find discussion topics of mutual interest. He was not satisfied in his secondary role after having been a governor of a very important state.

Crediting Lois Kinsey Marshall, wife of Thomas R. Marshall, Vice President with President Woodrow Wilson, with help on adjustment to the social life and ways of the high and mighty was typical of Grace Coolidge. Mrs. Marshall's "friendly guidance" made such a difference.[36] She took Grace to her first Ladies of the Senate luncheon and then invited those attending back to her apartment for a second meeting of these spouses and hostesses of U.S. Senators. Grace had little experience in this type of entertaining in Northampton or Boston. Grace soon learned that she was to "receive" on Wednesday afternoons with an open invitation to the public with tea and cakes flowing. Her first reception was for the diplomatic corps. It was a great success.

---

[32] Ross, p. 62.
[33] Fuess, p. 286.
[34] Ibid, p. 287.
[35] Ibid.
[36] *Grace Coolidge: An Autobiography*, p. 55.

The boys returned to Northampton to finish their school year after the inauguration. This was about four months without a parent and only a housekeeper in the house. Calvin was concerned about the boys and wrote his father, "I want you to go down to Northampton and stay with them three or four days and see that their clothes are all right, and their shoes and rubbers are all right. I hope this won't seem too burdensome to you."[37] Calvin asked his father to see their teachers due to John's poor Latin grade and Calvin Jr.'s deportment. Grace was also to spend two weeks back in Northampton. The boys seemed to bounce back with John improving in Latin and Calvin Jr. with "a fine card this month."[38] Grace was trying to help her husband in his new job, but an unintended result was that the boys were left on their own more than either parent had wanted.

Grace and Calvin were searching to find a school for the next year for both boys. They could not afford fancy preparatory schools in New England and wanted the boys closer to Washington, even in driving distance. They also wanted a school with a mission to instill public service and the morals and ethics which they had learned at a young age at home. Calvin wanted to move his father temporarily to Northampton to care for them.[39] Grace openly admitted, "The hardest thing for me in going to Washington was seeing less of my boys..."[40] She also missed New England where she loved "every stick and stone."[41] She discussed prep schools with Dean Olds in Northampton but he suggested Phillips-Andover which was too far away from Washington.[42] Frank Stearns wrote Dwight Morrow about the boys, and Calvin and Grace's dilemma. "He is very loathe to take them out of the public schools but I see no other way and I think he sees no other way under the circumstances. The boys are getting too old now to make it wise to have them under the sole supervision of the housekeeper. While they were quite small it worked very well, for the woman is conscientious and competent, but they must be somewhere where they are under the supervision of men and they will probably be sent to a private school."[43]

"A great responsibility rests upon us" wrote Grace Coolidge to Frank Stearns on May 25, 1921.[44] Here they were in Washington and her husband was having a difficult time adjusting. Her social skills saved many a dinner or party from

---

[37] *Your Son, Calvin Coolidge*, March 24, 1921, p.179.
[38] Ibid., p. 181.
[39] Ibid., p. 182.
[40] Round Robin letter, August 14, 1921 from Grace Coolidge, Pi Beta Phi Archives.
[41] Ibid.
[42] Grace Coolidge to Frank W. Stearns, May 25, 1921, Stearns Collection.
[43] Frank W. Stearns to Dwight Morrow, June 13, 1921, Stearns Collection.
[44] Ibid.

becoming awkward. She was without her Northampton friends, but she was to make new Washington friends and create conversations so that her silent partner husband would be accepted or at least tolerated. One day, when her husband was under the weather, she represented him in a program where President Harding gave a gram of radium to Madame Curie.[45] By December the Vice President was finally adjusting to the social scene. "In the smoking room Calvin gave every man an opportunity to talk with him and after he came into the drawing room he went around and talked to each woman in turn," she wrote a Northampton friend.[46] "The Vice President and his wife were social as well as political personages, entitled to precedence at dinners and regarded as 'lions' to be secured or celebrities at dinner parties."[47] This couple was now in demand on the Washington political and social scene.

The tone of the new Harding administration was actually set by Ned and Evalyn McLean, who hosted a private ball as a celebration of the inauguration at their estate, Friendship. Grace and Calvin joined in and watched the Hardings relish their newly won prestige. The lavish Georgian Revival house was built in northwest Washington on 43 acres with an 18 hole golf course, cast iron swimming pool, tennis courts, stables, Italian gardens, giant fountains and other luxuries.[48] The Duchess, as Florence Harding was called by many, "trusted and depended upon Evalyn."[49] Evalyn's devotion to disabled veterans from World War I became Mrs. Harding's cause as well. Despite the friendship of the millionaire couple, capital society often treated the Hardings with disdain.[50] That did not stop the Hardings from becoming very popular with the "common" people. The White House was open to the public for the first time since 1917. "Masses swarmed across the lawn and headed up to the house, even automobiles pulled up in the driveway."[51] Mrs. Harding ordered drinking fountains for the grounds and birdhouses for the trees. She even gave tours of the White House to tourists herself! Reporters were among the invited guests to state dinners.[52]

Mrs. Harding was "obsessed about her appearance, favoring beads, sparkles and spangles, flashing when she turned."[53] She often wore white satin with

---

[45] Grace Coolidge to Mrs. R.B. Hills, May 26, 1921, Coolidge Papers, Forbes Library.
[46] Ibid, December 29, 1921.
[47] Fuess, p. 287.
[48] Website, The Ballroom at McLean Gardens
[49] Carl Sferrazza Anthony, *Florence Harding, the First Lady, the Jazz Age, and the Death of America's Most Scandalous President* (New York: William Morrow and Company, 1998) p. 241.
[50] Ibid., p. 275.
[51] Ibid., p. 263.
[52] Ibid., p. 267.
[53] Anthony, p. 272.

countless streamers hanging from her waist, studded with jewels. She chose "delphinium-inspired blue-violet" for her gowns with matching bouquets or corsages. Fashionable people called the color "Duchess Blue" in her honor.[54] Her skirts were 8 inches from the ground. She wore a black velvet neckband with a diamond sunburst on it. It was her trademark and covered the wrinkles on her neck.[55] She was 60 years old and needed to dress up to outshine the much younger women around her. The second lady, Grace, was only forty two years old.

In 1921, women's skirts were much shorter than before, often only to the knee. Flappers wore short skirts which "flapped against their thighs."[56] Mrs. Harding's closest friend, Evalyn McLean, wore "dangerously plunging backlines that nearly reached the derriere."[57]

Like the Coolidges, the Hardings did not come from the high society of New York or Washington, but Mrs. Harding was the daughter of the richest man in Marion, Ohio and was brought up in a "setting of wealth, position, and privilege."[58] When she and Warren arrived in Washington in 1916 for his Senate position, she was a "strainer." She "strained to get up there! Social ambition," noted Lillian Parks, an observer from the downstairs at the White House. Only with Evalyn McLean's friendship did the First Lady finally have almost a younger sister and someone to sponsor her in society. Florence Harding had found the Senate social life to be entertaining. She poured the drinks, despite Prohibition, and encouraged the card games. She thought this would continue on at the White House as well. And it did.

Mrs. Harding had been "the boss" of the campaign to make Warren G. Harding a U.S. President. This victory was hers as much as his. As they entered the White House, she asked her husband, "Warren Harding, I have got you the Presidency. What are you going to do with it?" He replied, "May God help me, for I need it."[59] On his first day in the Oval Office, Florence was there when he arrived with a flower to go on his desk. "It was time for them to get to work."[60] She was the one who debated Senators such as Henry Cabot Lodge with President Harding acting as the referee.[61] She liked the game of politics.

The relationship of Florence Harding and her Second Lady, Grace Coolidge, was strained from the start. On November 4, 1920, Grace wrote Mrs. Harding

---

[54] Ibid, p. 273.
[55] Ibid, p. 251.
[56] Ibid., p. 272.
[57] Ibid., p. 252.
[58] Website, The White House, biography of Florence Harding
[59] Anthony, p. 261.
[60] Ibid., p. 264.
[61] Ibid.p. 337.

congratulations on the election with these words: "I am sure that you contributed in a very large measure to your husband's splendid victory....Please accept my very heartiest assurances of loyalty and support at all times."[62] The reply: "Your very charming letter of the morning after the election, breathing friendship and loyalty, pleased me, and heartened me, as my mind was projected into that future which is before us both...we shall both be able to work shoulder to shoulder with our husbands in the tremendous undertaking which lies just ahead."[63] On January 10, 1921, Grace wrote Mrs. Harding "to give me an idea of just how elaborate a gown you are to wear to the Inaugural Ball..."[64] Since an official ball was cancelled, Mrs. Harding lashed back and wrote, "I shall have nothing in the way of an inaugural gown."[65] She was going to New York and "what I get will be for general wear and purposes....It does simplify for us, doesn't it?"[66] Capital society often preferred the second lady, not the older bossy first lady.[67] Outward appearances were smooth. Only once did the tension between the First Lady and the Coolidges come to the surface. When Mrs. John B. Henderson, widow of a Missouri Senator, offered her house and grounds for the Vice Presidential couple in 1922, Congress was to accept the gift and make an appropriation for maintenance.[68] Dr. Butler, a politician visiting the White House, heard Florence shout, "Not a bit of it, not a bit of it. I am going to have that bill defeated. Do you think I am going to have those Coolidges living in a house like that? An hotel apartment is plenty good enough for them."[69]

Florence Harding often sent Grace Coolidge to functions in her stead when she was ill, which was often. Grace had her own round of social obligations "for teas, benefits, balls, receptions, dinners and concerts" and took on these additional assignments.[70] To improve her skills, she went to dancing class even though her husband did not dance. Thousands of callers took the opportunity to taste at the tea table at the Hotel Willard, their residence. Florence Harding's good friend, Evalyn McLean, threw a dinner party for the Coolidges with a film of the

---

[62] Letter from Grace Coolidge to Florence Harding, Florence Harding Papers, The Ohio Historical Society, Columbus, Ohio.
[63] Letter from Florence Harding to Grace Coolidge, November 11, 1920, Florence Harding Papers.
[64] Letter from Grace Coolidge to Florence Harding, January 10, 1921, Florence Harding Papers.
[65] Letter from Florence Harding to Grace Coolidge, January 12, 1921, Florence Harding Papers.
[66] Ibid.
[67] Anthony, p. 275.
[68] Ross, p. 63.
[69] Ibid., p. 64.
[70] Ibid., p. 65.

Dempsey-Carpentier fight on an outdoor movie screen so even Florence's best friend wanted to include these new personages to Washington.[71]

When leaders from nine nations came to Washington for the Conference on the Limitation of Armaments in the winter of 1921-1922, Florence saw to it that women were part of the action. President Harding opened the event with a speech including the spirited line, "We want less of armament and none of war!"[72] Florence Harding chose the women for her box at the conference: Mrs. Coolidge, Mrs. Taft, Mrs. Gillett, Mrs. Weeks and Mrs. Denby.[73] Grace attended the first and third of the plenary sessions with her knitting needles racing along, and dined in company with men such as Arthur Balfour and Lord Beatty. She enjoyed the conversation and added her pleasant comments and lovely demeanor to the gathering. Florence Harding thought White House dinners and social engagements brought "a common understanding" among the representatives.[74] After a year in office, Mrs. Harding even received her "own admiring editorial, 'Mrs. Harding's First Year in Office'."[75]

If Mrs. Harding had had her way, Calvin Coolidge would have been replaced on the ticket for the 1924 campaign. In her correspondence of April 25, 1923, a letter from Warren's cousin suggested that "From the present viewpoint Governor Lowden would be more helpful than anyone whose name has been mentioned."[76] Florence, the political pro, knew that a Midwesterner with support from farmers would be a better choice. Florence also planned an extensive trip out West to promote her husband. "Out West they don't know they have a President, and I am anxious to have them see Mr. Harding, which is one of the reasons for our trip."[77] She also wanted to get Warren away from his office work and his battles with the Senate. Warren wrote, "I never find myself done. I never find myself with my work completed. I don't believe there is a human being who can do all the work there is to be done in the President's office. It seems as though I have been President for twenty years."[78] He had only been in office one year. "By late spring [of 1923] it was obvious to all those around him that Harding was ill. His normal

---

[71] Ibid, p. 66.
[72] Anthony, p. 348.
[73] Florence Harding Papers #0496
[74] Ibid., p. 349.
[75] Ibid., p. 352.
[76] Florence Harding's Papers, Lucien E. Harding.
[77] Aunt Nellie from Florence Harding, February 13, 1923, Florence Harding Papers.
[78] Warren Harding Papers, New York Times March 5, 1922, quoted in Robert K. Murray, *The Harding Era, Warren G. Harding and His Administration* (Minneapolis: University of Minnesota Press, 1969), p. 417.

ruddy color had become a pallor and his energies were always at low ebb."[79] Even so he agreed with politicians in his party that a trip would be good and he loved to give speeches. Florence was worried and instructed presidential doctors General Sawyer and Captain Boone "to be as close to the President's room as possible."[80]

During these years in Washington, Grace had been preoccupied with the health of her own father and her family in Vermont. She traveled to be with him in Burlington and was worried about his physical deterioration. "Father's mind is hazy most of the time."[81] "Father needs more expert care than I could give him."[82] She did not expect him to live very much longer. Andrew died on April 25, 1923. After the funeral, she turned to her mother and her needs. One of the first decisions was to decide where her mother would live. For better care, in the fall, Mother Goodhue would move to the two family house in Northampton that Calvin and Grace called their official residence with the household assistance of Alice Reckahn.

The boys began Mercersburg Academy, a preparatory school about an hour from Washington in a rural town in Pennsylvania, in the fall of 1921. Dr. Joel Boone, the Assistant White House Physician, was a Mercersburg alumnus and encouraged the Vice Presidential couple to consider the school for their sons. Packing the same trunk that their father, Calvin, had used to go to Amherst College in 1891, the boys set off. Grace was pleased with the school and wrote the headmaster in April of 1922, "The boys write very cheerful letters. It means everything to me to know that they are happy and so well cared for."[83] As they headed for the summer of 1923, plans were made for both boys. John, 16 years old, was to attend Camp Devens, a military training camp for boys. Calvin Jr., age 15, set his own plan of harvesting tobacco in Northampton, Massachusetts. He would be very independent biking to his place of work and being watched over by the housekeeper. Both boys traveled with their parents to Plymouth, Vermont on July 8th in 1923 to visit their paternal grandfather. It was a thrill to take turns riding in the front seat with the driver of the Pierce Arrow. The boys would soon leave with the chauffeur to take a train to their summer destinations.[84] Grace packed them up with confidence that their summers would strengthen them and prepare them to be model boys for the nation.

---

[79] Ibid., p. 439.
[80] Ibid., p. 440.
[81] Grace Coolidge to Teresa Hills, February 6, 1923, Forbes Collection
[82] Ibid., March 3, 1923.
[83] Grace Coolidge to Dr. Irvine, April 27, 1922, Mercersburg Academy Archives, Mercersburg Academy, Mercersburg, Pennsylvania.
[84] Jim Cooke, "Dramatis Personae: Plymouth Notch, Vermont, Thursday-Friday, August 2-3, 1923" *The Real Calvin Coolidge #13*, (1998) p. 18.

The Vermont Standard of July 31, 1923 reported, "The optimistic tone of the bulletins from the bedside of President Harding—ill with pneumonia at the Palace Hotel in San Francisco—which are being received here tonight by Vice President Calvin Coolidge, have greatly relieved the tension under which the vice president has been laboring and he has decided to remain at Plymouth with his family for the next few days..."[85] The newspaper also reported that "metropolitan" journalists were headquartered in Woodstock "to be in easy reach of the man of the hour."[86] On July 29th, President Harding walked unaided to a car which drove him to the Palace Hotel in San Francisco. He rested in bed and "it was abundantly clear that Harding had had a cardiac collapse....it was also quickly determined that the president had bronchopneumonia."[87] On August 2nd, Warren was listening to his wife read from *The Saturday Evening Post,* he "twisted convulsively" and died.[88]

On the East Coast, the Coolidges had retired for the night to their simple room at the homestead in Plymouth, when Calvin's father came up the stairs calling his name. "I noticed that his voice trembled. As the only times I had ever observed that before were when death had visited our family, I knew that something of the gravest nature had occurred," wrote Calvin Coolidge.[89] Both of them prayed and Grace "wept quietly."[90] Grace and Calvin dressed immediately and read the message from George B. Christian, secretary to President Harding. A telegram was also driven to Plymouth with a message from Attorney General Harry M. Daugherty "advising the vice president to qualify as president with as little delay as possible."[91] Calvin and Grace both sent a telegram to Mrs. Harding offering their sympathies. Calvin and his father found a copy of the constitution and the oath was typed by Erwin C. Geisser, stenographer, who had arrived from nearby Bridgewater, Vermont. Grace brought in an oil lamp and then a second one so that her husband could work with his secretary in the parlor. After a statement was typed for the press, she distributed it. The reporters raced off with this, leaving only one reporter to take in the swearing in ceremony of the father, a notary public, giving the oath of office to his son. That was the scene that resonated with the public. The simple farmhouse in Vermont without a phone, central heating, electricity or indoor plumbing was the scene of the swearing in of

---

[85] Cyndy Bittinger, "The Tiny Hamlet of Plymouth Notch Becomes Nationally Known During Coolidge Term", *The Vermont Standard Sesquicentennial Edition*, October 30, 2003, p. 9C.
[86] Ibid.
[87] Murray, p. 449.
[88] Ibid., p. 450.
[89] Coolidge, p. 173-174.
[90] Ross, p. 77.
[91] Cooke, p. 22.

a president. And the official swearing him in was his father! Grace Coolidge was the only woman in the room and from this time on was to be there for him and the country just as she was during the vice presidential years.

Chapter 6

THE WHITE HOUSE YEARS

"...this was I and yet not I, this was the wife of the President of the United States and she took precedence over me; my personal likes and dislikes must be subordinated to the consideration of those things which were required of her."[1]

SETTING THE TONE

Calvin Coolidge, in his first statement to the public after he learned that President Harding had died, wrote, "It will be my purpose to carry out the policies which he has begun for the service of the American people and for meeting their responsibilities wherever they may arise."[2] Grace was to take a serious tone as well, but Florence Harding had broken the mold of past First Ladies. She spoke to the press, she debated politicians, she even ran Warren's campaign and was getting ready to do it again. Grace did not want to undo the popular policies of her predecessor, but she had to think of what was called for after the death of a popular president and what traditions she could resurrect that she and the nation would find comforting and reassuring during this decade of dramatic cultural and social change. Also the Hardings had openly flaunted the stated morality of the times. Liquor and poker had punctuated high times; showgirls were made available to male politicians in love nests. The New England parlor would be the model for the White House with this new, very proper presidential couple who obeyed the law of Prohibition.

---

[1] *Grace Coolidge: An Autobiography*, p. 62.
[2] Cooke, p. 22.

Back from Vermont, Grace met Florence Harding at the station upon her return to Washington and drove with her to the White House.[3] The couple gave Mrs. Harding all the time she needed to pack up her possessions at the White House and "cull the President's papers."[4] She spent a week there and then moved to Friendship, the McLean estate, and on September 5th left for Marion, Ohio.[5] Even though she moved back to the capital in the winter of 1923, she was no longer the focus of power in Washington. Calvin Coolidge told the chief usher, Ike Hoover, "I want things as they used to be—before!"[6] Grace Coolidge began her first day at the White House with a letter to her Pi Beta Phi Round Robin friends. She wrote,

> "I thought maybe you'd all like my contribution to be the first letter I wrote in the White House. Just now it occurred to me that I would begin my letter here in the only home I have known in Washington, take it with me as I go and finish it in that great White House on Pennsylvania Avenue—one which must now become home to me for a year and a half. I wish I could tell you all that is in my heart at this moment—but there is so much that even I am bewildered. I want you all to love me and pray for me."[7]

She continued in the letter to call herself "Alice in Wonderland or Babe in the Woods" knowing that she had a lot to learn. Mr. Stearns was their only guest at that time in the White House. This was appropriate since he was Coolidge's first backer in the quest for higher political offices and the rewards of this moment would be shared with him.

The first priority as a couple was to comfort Mrs. Harding and reassure the nation. At the age of 44, Grace had recently lost her father and consoled her mother. She was the mother of two sons and the wife of a man who channeled most of his familial devotion to her. Calvin had lost his mother, step mother, and sister. He was familiar with grief and sorrow. The second priority for her husband was to lead the nation. Grace knew to subordinate herself to the new role that her husband had suddenly gained. His decisions would impact her but she really could not object. She would need to find a way to help things go smoothly, seamlessly. She would also make contributions but they could not be controversial or adversarial. She had seen how Florence Harding ran Warren around. That she would never do.

---

[3] William Seale, *The President's House, A History* (New York: Harry N. Abrams, 1986) p. 853.
[4] Ibid.
[5] Murray, p. 485.
[6] Ibid., p. 500.

Regular White House entertainments were canceled during the mourning period of 90 days. Also new privacy rules had to be instituted. Newspapermen were to leave the boys alone. John and Calvin Jr. at Mercersburg Academy were not to be spied upon. The boys were 17 and 15 years old and "the first teenage children of a President to live in the White House since Charlie Taft moved out a decade before."[8] Grace wished she could visit her friends in Northampton before the boys went back to school but she wrote "I must not forget that I am to be guided now by circumstances beyond my control."[9] She continued in a letter to Mrs. Hills, "Be waiting for me when my turn of service is over. I go into it determined to do everything in my power to help, humbly, praying for guidance and strength. The absolute rest of the past four weeks means much to Calvin now and he has stood up under all this sudden change caused by the removal of the President amazingly well."[10]

Grace had not become well acquainted with all the Cabinet officers during her short time in Washington. She was however, "closely associated with their wives" and had tea with them in the "drawing room on the second floor of the White House once a month" and they "discussed subjects of interest to social Washington."[11] Thus Grace was in the social mix. She also swam quite often at Friendship, the McLean's Washington home, so was bound to be part of that social circle to a degree.

The Washington bureaucracy continued to function no matter who was in the White House. Since Grace Coolidge found entertaining fun and uplifting, she was a perfect one to take over the social aspects of the first ladyship. When the mourning period was over at the end of September, Grace received a delegation from the Red Cross Convention. The staff worked with the first lady to hold four state dinners and four musicales in her first winter at the White House. In addition there were "five large receptions; two musicales during Lent; and several garden parties in late April or early May."[12] For these receptions, the president and first lady walked to the Blue Room with Cabinet members and their wives following while the Marine Band played "Hail to the Chief." Edmund Starling, the secret serviceman guarding President Coolidge, compared the Coolidges to other White House couples. "The Coolidges made their formal bow as White House host and hostess that winter and were amazingly successful, being gracious and friendly

---

[7] Grace Coolidge to Pi Beta Phi Round Robins, August 21, 1923, Pi Beta Phi Archives.
[8] Seale, p. 857.
[9] Grace Coolidge to Mrs. Teresa Hills, August 5, 1923, Forbes Library.
[10] Ibid.
[11] *The Real Calvin Coolidge #1*, p. 25
[12] Seale, p. 858.

without ostentation or flurry."[13] "Mrs. Coolidge was the personification of charm. She more than made up for her husband's taciturnity. Everyone liked her, and she carried off the difficult role of first lady beautifully. Without her the little fellow would have had a difficult time at the dinners, receptions, and balls which custom forced him to attend," added Starling.[14] At receptions, the couple "stood at the south end of the Blue Room, receiving a moving line of people that snaked across the entrance hall to the State Dining Room, and on around through the Red Room....The crowds at receptions were so thick that on hot days both hosts and guests experienced considerable misery."[15] However the Coolidges "received universal acclaim for their performances in the social season of 1923-24."[16]

Grace was pleased to hold garden parties since she enjoyed music and meeting people. When she received people in the East Room, the Marine Band played on the terrace just outside. She also gave musicales in the East Room. Guests sat on small gilt chairs for the entertainment after dinner. For instance in the month of March, 1924, "Sergei Rachmaninoff, Salzedo, Greta Torpadie, Marguerite D'Alvarez, John Barclay, John Charles Thomas, and the twenty-year-old violinist Erica Morini all appeared on the Lenten musicale series."[17] Grace's interest in music extended beyond the White House. She was "honorary chair of the World Fellowship through Music Convention" and welcomed many choirs to the White House after their performances in the city.[18] "The president saw these musical ensembles as a direct link with the nation's universities, religious organizations, and diverse population."[19] Colleges sent their choirs, even the choir from President's college, Amherst College, came.

A typical day for Grace included appointments to meet her at twelve noon, followed by pictures at the stone steps on the south portico of the White House.[20] Tea for about 25 people was arranged twice a week in the Red Parlor. An aide made the introductions and a friend poured the tea.[21] Reporters wanted to interview the First Lady, but "it [was her] unbroken policy not to see newspaper

---

[13] Col. Edmund W. Starling, *Starling of the White House, The Story of the Man Whose Secret Service Detail Guarded Five Presidents from Woodrow Wilson to Franklin D. Roosevelt* (New York: Simon and Schuster, 1946) p.219.
[14] Ibid.
[15] Seale, p. 859.
[16] Ibid.
[17] Elise K. Kirk, *Music at the White House, A History of the American Spirit* (Urbana and Chicago: University of Illinois Press, 1986) p. 210.
[18] Ibid, p. 208.
[19] Ibid:, p. 214.
[20] *Grace Coolidge: An Autobiography*, p. 68.
[21] Ibid, p. 69.

writers or give interviews to anyone. At the word interview spoken or written my ears go up and my chin out," she once wrote a friend.[22]

Grace thought she could get exercise by horseback riding since her sons and husband already had made use of the White House stables. She was a modern woman of the twenties and wanted to try sports such as swimming and horse back riding. She secretly planned to start riding with the assistance of Dwight Davis, the Assistant Secretary of War. However reporters spied her and the story of her ride landed on the front page of the Washington newspapers; the President ended her fun with the comment, "I think you will find that you will get along at this job fully as well if you do not try anything new."[23] Her secret plan backfired. The family was closely watched and now she was caught by the press and her husband did not even know this was coming. Also there could have been a touch of jealousy by her husband since women rarely wore pants in public and here she was out of her normal roles of hostess, mother, or wife. The President also did not encourage her dancing with anyone but their sons' friends. He offered Grace rides on his new mechanical horse in the privacy of their rooms.[24] She regularly took a brisk walk during the forenoon. One of her favorite walks was around the reflecting basin in front of the Lincoln Memorial.[25] She realized that exercise was important and did not think her new role precluded this important part of her day. This was a very modern attitude.

In terms of their personal lives, the staff was unanimous on one observation: Calvin Coolidge adored his wife. Frank Stearns, Calvin's mentor, told Starling, "...in all things Mrs. Coolidge came first—something [he] found to be true without exception."[26] Lillian Parks, daughter of a maid in the White House, reported that Calvin "worshipped his wife" shopping for "the most luxurious gowns he could find" for her and did not want to acknowledge anyone who "neglected her" before they were president and First Lady.[27]

Grace was really a "government worker" as she once called herself. She did not know her schedule on many of the days at the White House. Grace, in her letters to friends, constantly commented that life was hard to plan without much advance information from her spouse. After two weeks at the White House, Grace asked for a schedule and her husband's now famous reply was, "Grace, we don't

---

[22] Grace Coolidge to Teresa Hills, April 6, 1927, Forbes Library.
[23] *The Real Calvin Coolidge #3*, p. 11.
[24] Ross, p. 98.
[25] *Grace Coolidge: An Autobiography*, p. 68.
[26] Starling, p. 234.
[27] Lillian Rogers Parks, *My Thirty Years Backstairs at the White House* (New York: Fleet Publishing Corp., 1961) p. 183-184.

give that out conspicuously."[28] Grace was not to inquire about policy or programs, but she was to accept her husband's intense interest in the inner workings of the White House day that a first lady traditionally ran. In past administrations, the housekeeper and first lady usually planned the meals. Now menus were to be cleared with the President every morning as well.[29] The menus for the day were sent to the couple "with the breakfast trays" and they made any changes.[30] Then the housekeeper went off to market in a horse drawn carriage with these instructions. "For the first time, a First Lady did not bring any servants with her, and the story went around backstairs that Mrs. Coolidge was used to doing all her own housework."[31] Often the first couple of the nation was wealthy and had staff or servants at their mansions or plantations back home. This New England couple, who had one housekeeper in Northampton, now found themselves with 18 servants, special cleaning men, a valet for the president and a maid for the first lady.[32]

When Florence Harding was packing to leave the White House, she introduced Mrs. Jaffray, head housekeeper, to Grace Coolidge with the advice to follow the housekeeper's direction. This was Florence Harding at her worst, assuming that Grace, coming to the White House without servants, would not know what to do. Mrs. Harding said, "I hope Mrs. Jaffray will like you." Mrs. Jaffray said, "My dear Mrs. Harding, it isn't a question of whether I like Mrs. Coolidge but of whether Mrs. Coolidge likes me." Mrs. Jaffrey was taken by Grace right away when Grace said, "I would like, Mrs. Jaffray, for everything to go on just as it has in the past."[33]

Mrs. Jaffrey continued on but found her new boss, Calvin Coolidge, wanting a strict budget for food for themselves, their guests, and the staff. This was his only expense and he wanted to cut it! Mrs. Jaffrey did understand that presidents had no retirement pensions and thus either had to save money at the White House or find a job when they retired from this one! Mrs. Jaffrey must have cut quite an image still traveling by a horse drawn coach to buy food at the market! She also took pride in finding food that President Coolidge actually liked! He evidently was a hard one to please.

Mrs. Jaffrey left in 1926 and Frank Stearns found a housekeeper Grace could count on. This was not a staff member whom she had inherited from the prior

---

[28] Ross, p. 98.
[29] Parks, p. 181.
[30] *Grace Coolidge: An Autobiography*, p. 63.
[31] Parks, p. 175.
[32] Ross, p. 97.
[33] Elizabeth Jaffray, *Secrets of the White House* (New York: Cosmopolitan Book Corp, 1926) p. 97.

administrations. On May 10, 1926, she wrote Miss Riley, before she was hired, "It has seemed to me that that department of the household was not well systematized and I would like to put someone in charge of it who would look after its varied details in a way that would relieve me of that responsibility. It seems to me that it is one of the most important and interesting posts in the establishment."[34]

Grace Coolidge had routines she followed and she tried to keep to them at the White House. As biographer Carl Anthony observed, she was a very sensual woman. She liked to use all her senses. "Music from the radio or Victrola, in which [her] canaries joined" accompanied her as she arranged flowers and waited for her secretary to arrive and open and classify the mail in the morning.[35] Now Grace needed a second secretary, so she hired Miss Mary Randolph. She needed someone at her telephone all day long. Miss Harlan, who had been a secretary to Florence Harding, and Miss Randolph took turns going to lunch.[36] The categories for the mail were: "personal, requests to be received, requests for donations and articles for bazaars, requests for photographs and autographs, requests for assistance of various sorts, invitations to be present at meetings or ceremonies of one kind or another, and letters from persons of unsound minds which were turned over to the Secret Service."[37]

Grace Coolidge had to decide how much entertaining they would do. Florence Harding had presented a boisterous, hip White House with wild times competing with time for political decisions. Of course Florence received the diplomats and Congressmen, but the stability of family life never seemed to matter that much to her. Grace was to "cling to the old way...and being the President's wife isn't going to make me think less about domestic things I've always loved."[38] She wanted to spend time with her boys whenever they were there on vacations from boarding school, and she wanted to keep her hobbies and interests going.

She had always made her own dresses, often augmented by store bought gowns. Even in the White House, she continued to sew and wrote of this activity to her friends in Northampton. Her husband "urged her to abandon her plain cottons and woolens and buy dresses with rhinestones, feathers, and fur."[39] He often shopped for her on his walks around Washington. Grace Coolidge was

---

[34] Grace Coolidge to Ellen Riley, Riley Papers, Vermont Division for Historic Preservation, Plymouth, Vermont.
[35] Ibid, p. 65-66.
[36] Grace Coolidge to Mrs. Teresa Hills, December of 1923, Forbes Library.
[37] *Grace Coolidge: An Autobiography*, p. 66.
[38] Ross, p. 89.
[39] Seale, p. 856.

"modern without being vulgar."[40] Calvin disapproved of slacks or culottes. She did not wear pants in public until after he died. Housekeeper Maggie Rogers told her daughter that "she was his queen, and he wanted to give her everything and do everything for her."[41]

She did not wear the flapper style skirts but "used primary colors, white cottons, and light pastels in flat-chested, low-hipped dresses."[42] Her hats were tight-fitting cloche or wide brim. Evening dresses were "long-trained brocades of gold, silver, white, and red. Sparkled belts and fans, fur pieces, rhinestone shoe buckles..." and all were the subject of the women's page editors who wrote about her.[43] Grace Coolidge was a conscious "fashion leader."[44] Red was her color.[45]

Since Grace did not speak to the press or accept interviews, her clothing and the settings where chosen carefully to show off her beauty and her sense of fashion. For a musicale in December of 1923, Mrs. Coolidge wore "a lovely draped gown of cloth of gold, with roses woven into the material in Persian colors. It was made with a square neck and narrow shoulder straps, and had paneled court train."[46] In March of 1924, at one of her Lenten musicales in the East Room of the White House, she wore a "gown of champagne silk crepe, made on straight lines."[47] Also, in April of 1924, Mrs. Coolidge wore a white satin brocade gown at her first official reception at the White House and she gave the dress to the New National Museum in tribute to the Pi Beta Phi fraternity who had visited. In May when they entertained 1,600 guests of official, diplomatic and resident Washington, Mrs. Coolidge wore a silk shawl of "Roman stripes" over a "costume of café-au-lait chiffon made on straight lines and combined effectively with heavy lace of the same shade. Her hat was a large picture one of brown lace with a brown bow of lace at one side."[48] When socializing with the Women's Press Club that month she also sported a new pin in the shape of an American eagle with diamonds, rubies, and sapphires in the design.[49] At the end of May for a garden party, Mrs. Coolidge stood at the east room near the head of the grand staircase. She wore "a gown of Lanvin green chiffon, embroidered with a flower

---

[40] Carl Sferrazza Anthony, *First Ladies, The Saga of the Presidents' Wives and Their Power, 1789-1961* (New York: William Morrow, 1990), p. 409
[41] Parks, p. 183.
[42] Ibid.
[43] Ibid.
[44] Ibid., p. 410.
[45] (Her dress is red in the Howard Chandler Christy painting and the dress given to the Smithsonian for the First Lady exhibit.)
[46] Hall, p. 17.
[47] Ibid., p. 34.
[48] Ibid., p.42.
[49] Ibid., p. 43.

design of the same shade, over a flesh colored slip. It was made with long waist and rather full skirt, with small French flowers in pastel shades marking the waist line. With this she wore a picture hat of white braid, ornamented at the left side with a single huge poppy."[50] These outfits spoke for her and the public swooned with approval.

Life was not all formality and no play. One time Wilson Brown, a naval aide, turned back to ask the Coolidges a question at the end of a reception. He caught a glimpse of "the President and his wife, believing themselves to be alone, solemnly dancing a minuet with exaggerated bows and curtsies."[51] They were having fun!

Grace Coolidge was a gracious hostess. The family had lots of visitors and she wrote Mrs. Hills, one of her best friends back in Northampton, "while I do not make their beds I have to make plans to keep them occupied for usually they have a lot of sight seeking to be done between meals. I am going now to the Senate luncheon."[52] She wrote Ivah Gale, her roommate from college, "This is a beautiful old house, Ivah, rich in memories and traditions. Those who live here are of necessity very much hemmed in by form and circumstance but there are many compensations."[53]

An account by French Strother, a magazine editor, described the couple on a typical evening. "The visitor is at once introduced to Mrs. Coolidge. A more complete contrast between two people, both in appearance and manner, would be hard to imagine. The President's very fair complexion, with the red showing very plainly through (he abundantly freckles in summer); his blue-gray eyes; his thin, straight, and sandy hair; his prominent nose, and slightly rounded shoulders, are in direct contrast to the corresponding features of Mrs. Coolidge. Her complexion is olive; her eyes large and dark brown; her hair abundant, wavy, black just lightly powdered with grey, her nose has an almost jaunty tilt, and her carriage is easy and erect."[54] Strother made it clear that, "The conversation is about anything and everything except the President's work. Never since her marriage has Mrs. Coolidge discussed his business with her husband."[55] She is a social being with "lively spirits, an irrepressible instinct for fun, a gift for ready and entertaining conversation, warmth of feeling and the capacity to express it..."[56] She made every effort to get her husband to relax and to have the guests try to do likewise.

---

[50] Ibid., p. 44
[51] Edward Connery Lathem, ed., *Meet Calvin Coolidge* (Brattleboro, Vermont: The Stephen Greene Press, 1960), p. 106.
[52] Grace Coolidge to Mrs. Teresa Hills, March 11, 1924, Forbes Library.
[53] Grace Coolidge to Ivah Gale, September 28, 1923, Ivah Gale Collection.
[54] Lathem, p. 91.
[55] Ibid., p. 92.
[56] Ibid.

An important role of the first couple is to receive foreign heads of state and other dignitaries. Grace "relished these brisk encounters with world figures more than her husband did."[57] Royalty from Europe wanted invitations to the White House. Queen Marie of Rumania, in 1926, started her visit with a ticket tape parade in New York City! "The Queen sparkled from her diamond and pearl diadem to her rhinestone-studded slippers."[58] "Miss Randolph brought up the guests in order of rank, four at a time, and they sat two by two in small gold chairs at either end of the sofa…"[59] Keeping the Queen from promoting herself was difficult. The Coolidges enjoyed Crown Prince Gustavus Adolphus of Sweden far more since he appreciated the city and wanted to understand American life. The Crown Prince of Japan visited as well as the Premier of France, the Governor-General of Canada, and the Presidents of the Irish Free State, Cuba, Haiti and Mexico. Mrs. Coolidge would receive the wives of the officials.

The only foreign travel they undertook was to Cuba in January of 1928 which was a success with over 80,000 cheering for them at the presidential palace in Havana.[60] President Coolidge was there to open the sixth Pan American Congress with twenty one countries participating. In November of 1928, diplomats from over 50 nations came to honor the Coolidges at a State reception led by the British ambassador.

Since Calvin Coolidge took great delight in the trappings of the office; Grace made the most of this. Both of them felt more comfortable in smaller groups where they could actually get to know people. They enjoyed taking a sail on the Presidential yacht *Mayflower* with its crew of seven officers and 142 men.[61] Life on the ship was formal with ladies in long dresses and gentlemen in tuxedos, but since only a small group could fit on the ship, no one felt excluded if they were not invited. When approaching Mt. Vernon, on the Potomac River, the Marine guard "appeared with rifles and presented arms, and the ship's complement stood at salute. The bell tolled, the band played "The Star-Spangled Banner," the bugler sounded "Taps," and the national colors were dipped."[62] The men appeared in "dress uniform, the crew manning the rail, band and Marine Guard paraded clear of the gangway, sideboys within hail, stewards on the dock ready to bring baggage on board for the passengers." Cabinet members were greeted by the bugle, ruffles and appropriate march. When the President came aboard the

---

[57] Ross, p. 106.
[58] Ross, p. 197.
[59] Ross, p. 198.
[60] Hall, p. 251.
[61] Milton F. Heller, Jr., *The President's Doctor, An Insider's View of Three First Families* (New York: Vantage Press, 2000) p. 35.

"Presidential flag would then be broken at the main truck, the gangway hauled aboard, lines cast off, and the *Mayflower* would steam majestically down river, graceful as a swan. The president would walk aft to greet his guests and sit with them for a time on deck..."[63] The head steward brought him his yachting cap. It was all very wonderful for a man who grew up in the woods of Vermont. It was the best part of socializing for the first lady.

The *Mayflower*'s medical officer and assistant physician at the White House was Joel T. Boone. He first met the Coolidges at the Willard Hotel for tea when Grace and Calvin were trying to decide where the boys should attend school during the Vice Presidential years. Boone suggested Mercersburg Academy in Mercersburg, Pennsylvania, of which he was an alumnus. Grace asked Boone to take them on a tour to see if the school would be a good choice. Boone was able to transmit his strong appreciation of the school to the Coolidge family.[64] When the boys were in Washington, Boone acted almost as an older brother for the boys. They "rode horseback, played tennis, shot pool, went sightseeing in Washington, and had lunch aboard the *Mayflower*" together.[65] To Dr. Boone each boy was so different. Calvin Jr. was "a sprightly lad with a fine sense of humor" and John "was a serious, hard-working young man, who was especially close to his mother."[66] Boone admired Grace Coolidge very much and was very much a confidant for her.

Grace tried to balance her devotion equally for both boys. Calvin Jr. had taught her to swim and thoroughly enjoyed sports as much as his mother did. He was adored by both his parents and admired by his older brother. His father wrote in his *Autobiography* that the boy showed "much promise, proficient in his studies, with a scholarly mind," at just 16 years old. "He had a remarkable insight into things," he wrote and then quoted the story that when Calvin Jr. learned of his father's elevation to the presidency in August of 1923 when the lad was harvesting tobacco in the fields of Massachusetts. "If my father was President I would not work in a tobacco field," a fellow laborer commented to Calvin Jr. "If my father were your father, you would," was the reply.[67] The boy resembled his grandmother, Victoria Josephine Moor Coolidge, with his fair coloring, blue eyes and light brown hair with glints of red. Calvin Jr. was sensitive and very much

---

[62] Ibid., p. 37.
[63] Lathem, p. 107.
[64] Milton F. Heller, Jr., "The Boones and the Coolidges," *The Real Calvin Coolidge #14*, p. 5.
[65] Ibid, p. 7.
[66] Ibid., p. 8.
[67] *The Autobiography of Calvin Coolidge*, pp. 189-190.

missed his mother when he first went to boarding school at the age of thirteen. In a letter of June, 1924 before school was out for the summer he wrote,

> "I felt pretty homesick after you left, mother, I have only been afflicted with that two or three times since I have been here. Strange to say I was'nt [sic] bothered at all when I first came here. Some boys leave because they get homesick when they come here. Doctor Irvine [the headmaster] says that kind of boys will run all the rest of their lives, but I think he is somewhat too broad in that statement."[68]

The headmaster observed that Calvin Jr. was like his father by being quiet and taciturn but under the exterior "there was fire and eagerness and tenderness, hidden from mere acquaintances but which won the love and admiration of all who knew him well."[69] Both boys "had outstanding academic records and their names were on the Honor Roll throughout their school years."[70] Calvin loved sports, especially tennis, track, baseball and horseback riding. He was a reporter for his school newspaper and an editor for the literary magazine as well as a fine debater.

Both boys worked on summer vacations from school. In later years, John Coolidge remembered his trips to Plymouth from Northampton, MA where he helped with haying, repairing buildings, and other odd jobs. Each had had a paper route in Northampton. When their father became president, John was at The Citizens' Military Training Camp, Camp Devens, in Ayer, Massachusetts.

Seriousness of life was instilled by their father. Religion was important to their mother and thus the boys were brought up in the Edwards Church in Northampton and the Coolidge parents were instrumental in the construction of a chapel at Mercersburg. Grace tried to lighten the atmosphere when they vacationed at the White House. The boys were squired around town by their mother to see historic sites and art galleries. In the summer, they were offered weekend trips on the *Mayflower*, swimming parties, horses from the White House stables, and use of the private tennis courts.

The First Lady ordered a beautiful Christmas tree for the Blue Room in the White House for December of 1923 and arranged for a magician to perform one day followed by informal dancing for the boys.[71] Discouraged by her husband

---

[68] Letter from Calvin Jr. to his mother at the White House, June 14, 1924, Calvin Coolidge Memorial Foundation archives, CCMF, Plymouth, Vermont
[69] Margaret Jane Fischer, *Calvin Coolidge, Jr.* (Rutland, VT: Academy Books, 1981) p.5.
[70] Ibid., p. 20.
[71] Ibid., p. 19.

from dancing with adults, she took the opportunity to dance with 60 boys in one evening. Grace and the boys decorated two trees, one for the family quarters. Grace felt that Christmas carols should be sung at the White House. She arranged for carols to be printed in the newspapers and 10,000 people came to the White House lawns to sing along with those who listened on the radio, probably over a million.[72] The first "National Christmas Tree" was lighted when "President Coolidge touched an electric button at its foot."[73]

President Calvin Coolidge and family, Grace, John, Calvin Jr. (CCMF archives)

---

[72] Mary Evans Seeley, *Season's Greetings from the White House* (New York: A Mastermedia Book, 1996) p. 11.
[73] Hall, *White House Days*, p. 22.

Both parents looked forward to visits from the boys. The two Calvins shopped together in December of 1923 and the boys received wonderful gifts for their first holiday in their new home. An article in the *Washington Post* humorously described the Santa Claus pack for the White House which should "include radio apparatus, airplane models, plenty of books, and a musical instrument or two if he wants to entirely please the young Mr. Coolidges."[74] The young men went with their parents to Walter Reed Hospital to visit injured men from the armed services and view a new film, "Abraham Lincoln." The boys went to the National Theatre to hear music and to see "Hamlet." During vacations, the family took advantage of plays and concerts to broaden the boys' education. They also had fun, even attending baseball games.

DEATH OF A SON

It was a challenge trying to bring the boys up with newspaper reporters looking at their every move. There were some things Grace did not want in the press and wanted to keep within the family. It was hard for them to live a normal life with so many people watching. In the summer of 1924, the boys had plans to attend Citizens Military Training Camp at Camp Devens, which John had attended in 1923, and to visit their 79 year old grandfather in Plymouth, Vermont. The first boys of the land were to set a good example for the nation.[75] Calvin Jr. once confided to Harry Vogel, an elevator operator at the New Willard Hotel, "I don't like living at the White House as well as at the hotel. There is too much company for meals."[76] The boy, according to Vogel, was "a regular boy, democratic and unspoiled."[77] It was said that "he had his mother's love for fun, her humor, and her quick wit, but he was still his father's son in many ways."[78]

On Monday, July 2, Dr. Joel T. Boone arrived to play tennis on the White House courts with the boys and Jim Haley of the Secret Service. He saw John playing tennis with Jim but no Calvin. When he inquired where Calvin was, he found him lying in the Lincoln bedroom with Mrs. Coolidge playing the piano nearby. Dr. Boone felt the boy's head and "found it was very hot" and then "found some swollen glands."[79] Calvin Jr. explained that he was in a hurry to play

---

[74] Ibid.
[75] personal interview with John Coolidge, 1999.
[76] Fischer, p. 14.
[77] Ibid.
[78] *Mercersburg Alumni Quarterly*, p. 58.
[79] Heller, p. 83.

tennis on Monday, and failed to wear socks and got a blister. Dr. Boone saw a "darker blister than one would ordinarily see...I then looked over his legs and found some red streaks. Then I knew we were in trouble."[80] Boone called Dr. Coupal, the White House physician, and they took a culture for the Naval Medical School laboratory. "Then they disclosed their apprehension to President and Mrs. Coolidge."[81] Grace Coolidge, as observed by her secretary Mary Randolph, "moved about the sickroom, quiet, efficient, resourceful. She could have the inexpressible comfort of being always with her child."[82] The next day, July 3, Boone and Coupal found that Calvin's illness was worse and asked Col. William Keller, chief of surgery at Walter Reed Army Hospital to confer with them. All three physicians were in the armed forces, so Boone sought civilian consultation. Dr. John B. Deaver, Professor of Surgery at the German Hospital in Philadelphia, came by train and was "suspicious of appendicitis." Meanwhile the culture from the laboratory showed "staphylococcus aureus."[83] On July 5th Dr. Deaver returned with Dr. Kolmar, a pathologist from the University of Pennsylvania, and they decided that Calvin should be moved to a hospital. Dr. Keller suggested Walter Reed Army Hospital and Calvin was taken there by ambulance. They decided to operate and made an incision over the left tibia and the culture showed "generalized staphylococcus aureo septicemia, or blood poisoning."[84]

John visited his brother in the hospital and returned shaken.[85] On July 6th the newspapers were alerted with an effort to find someone with Calvin's blood type for transfusions. The Coolidges stayed at Walter Reed in a room across the hall. On July 7th respiratory symptoms appeared and oxygen was administered to the sixteen year old lad. Boone observed that President Coolidge had pressed a locket into the hand of his son which contained a lock of his grandmother's hair. When the son dropped it, the father held it for him and caressed his forehead and brushed back his hair. Boone diagnosed an intestinal obstruction and the youth was overwhelmed with infection. His heart faltered and his pulse ceased. "No therapeutic measure then known to medical science was able to save this boy's life."[86] Only eight days had passed from that fateful tennis game.

Eight years later, in a personal letter to John, Grace wrote her view of events that day,

---

[80] Heller, p. 84.
[81] Ibid.
[82] Ibid.
[83] Heller, p. 85.
[84] Ibid.
[85] Fisher, p. 25.

"I leaned over his bed knowing that he was fast slipping beyond the reach of my voice, perhaps even then would not hear, and I said, "You're alright Calvin, as I had said it so many times in the days when he was trouble about some little matter. Without opening his eyes, he nodded his head, ever so little and the flicker of his old smile came and was gone. Then, they began giving him oxygen and kept his heart beating but his spirit had slipped away. All that afternoon, dark, awe-inspiring clouds had rolled across the sky, the lightening was almost constant and thunder followed it in mighty roars of majestic power. Calvin's delirium seemed to be a part of it all and, for a long time, he seemed to be on a horse leading a cavalry charge in battle. He called out, "Come on, come on, help, help!" And, for a time, he thought he was sitting backwards on his horse and asked us to turn him around. Father put his arms under him and tried to persuade him that he had turned him but he thought he was still wrong side around. Finally, he relaxed and called out, "We surrender, we surrender!" Dr. Boone said, "Never surrender, Calvin." He answered only, "Yes." And some how I was glad that he had gone down still fighting. After it was all over, Dr. Coupal broke down and cried. I found him at the window and I put my arms around him and told him that everything was alright that he and the other doctors had done everything within their power and we must comfort ourselves with the thought that courage such as Calvin had shown us all must now be our example."[87]

Mrs. Coolidge "gazed silently at her son in death. The two [parents] quietly left the death chamber, expressed their thanks to all who had attended Calvin, and returned to the White House."[88] Grace had been most stoic. She had been a nurse to her son and a worried mother. The presidential couple had looked to modern medicine to help them, but nothing had been invented yet to save their son. Grace wanted to be strong for her remaining son and husband. She also had her faith.

"The nation was stunned by this tragedy."[89] The Democratic convention adjourned. People of this era often remember where they were when this was announced just as people who lived during the 1960s remember where they were when President Kennedy was shot. Ten thousand telephone calls asking about Calvin Jr. were made to the White House. Fourteen thousand cards were mailed back to acknowledge the outpouring telegrams, letters, cards and floral pieces. No death ever generated such expression of sympathy up until this time.[90] *The Washington Post* of July 9th: "Calvin Coolidge, Jr., young son of the President and Mrs.Coolidge, sleeps peacefully in death in the east room of the White House, his

---

[86] Heller, p. 86.
[87] Grace Coolidge to John Coolidge, July, 1932, the Calvin Coolidge Memorial Collection.
[88] Ibid.
[89] Heller, p. 87.
[90] *The Mercersburg Academy Alumni Quarterly*, p. 57.

bier guarded by marines and sailors of the *U.S.S. Mayflower*, while ever-increasing bowers of floral tributes bespeaks the grief and fond remembrances of the Nation."[91] Calvin Jr. had enjoyed the *Mayflower* boat trips and the crew wished to participate in his memorial service. The White House grounds were opened for those who wished to come and honor his memory. "Mrs. Coolidge did not need the support of her husband and son. She walked with a firm and unhesitating step and with head erect. She seemed to have steeled herself. She wore a simple dress of severest black, but without hat or veil."[92] "Hundreds stood outside the open windows in the summer sunshine, as they would again stand in silence early that evening all along the route to the station as his body was borne to the funeral train that would take him back to New England."[93] Members of the cabinet and their wives joined the immediate family and close friends for the trip to Northampton, Massachusetts for services at the Congregational church there. Col. John Coolidge, his grandfather, and Lemira Goodhue, his maternal grandmother, joined the presidential family in Northampton. The train then left for Ludlow with many people standing along the tracks in tribute. The funeral party proceeded the last twelve miles by automobile with a cavalry escort. The last third of a mile troops of Boy Scouts stood in silence, each holding a rose. At the close of the service, they placed their flowers at the grave. As the casket was being lowered, Grace carefully put Calvin Jr.'s Bible upon it.[94]

Grace Coolidge later wrote of the final hours,

> "It is a beautiful spot and it was lovely the day we left little Calvin there. Before our train got to Ludlow there had been a thunderstorm-shower which laid the dust and made everything fresh and green. As we stood beside the grave the sun was shining, throwing long slanting shadows and the birds were singing their sleepy songs. Truly, it seemed to me God's Acre. There was a prayer, a few passages of scripture and two hymns, and the Mercersburg hymn which I have seen Calvin sing with the other boys at school and I could seem to hear and see him there. 'Taps' never sounded as it did there, echoing and re-echoing from mountain to mountain. I came away with a 'peace which passeth understanding,' comforted and full of courage."[95]

---

[91] Hall, p. 52.
[92] *The Mercersburg Academy Alumni Quarterly*, Vo. 20, January, 1925, No. 2, p. 47.
[93] Fischer, p. 30.
[94] *Alumni Quarterly*, p. 48.
[95] Ibid, p. 34

On the fifth anniversary of her son's death she wrote a poem which she did share with the nation as it was published in a magazine. The poem shows her faith which seemed to sustain her as she moved forward.

Open Door

You, my son,
Have shown me God.
Your kiss upon my cheek
Has made me feel the gentle touch
Of Him who leads us on.
The memory of your smile, when young,
Reveals His face,
As mellowing years come on apace.
And when you went before,
You left the Gates of Heaven ajar
That I might glimpse,
Approaching from afar,
The glories of His Grace.
Hold, son, my hand,
Guide me along the path,
That, coming,
I may stumble not,
Nor roam,
Nor fail to show the way
Which leads us—Home.[96]

All the Coolidges were shaken by this sudden death of such a young and promising son. Calvin, the father, blamed himself for this death. After all, he was president and the boys had access to tennis courts they never would have had if he had only been a governor. He did not know "why such a price was exacted for occupying the White House."[97] Political scientist Robert Gilbert has analyzed Coolidge as plunging into deep depression after the death of his son.[98] The Coolidges saw Mercersburg Academy as a place where the memory of Calvin Jr. could be preserved. They designated a gold cross for the altar of chapel inscribed with "The Most Precious Things to God" in Latin. A portrait of Calvin Jr. by Richard S. Meryman was prepared for the headmaster's office. Their older son,

---

[96] Fischer, p. 34.
[97] *The Autobiography of Calvin Coolidge*, p. 190.
[98] Robert E. Gilbert, *The Mortal Presidency: Illness and Anguish in the White House* (New York: Fordham University Press, 1998).

John, went to the school to retrieve the items stored over the summer for his brother. Grace wrote the wife of the headmaster in August of 1924, "You would have been surprised to see how carefully Calvin had packed away his bedding, his books and his treasures."[99] In June of 1925, Grace and her friend Teresa Hills visited the school and Grace expressed how moved she was to be there.

> "Always, I feel a beautiful sense of nearness to Calvin. Just as I used to share his happiness and his little disappointments, the stories that he read and the songs he sang, so now, I seem to glimpse a little of Heaven with him and wherever I visit the places that he frequented and am with the people whom he loved while he was there I know that in a very real sense we are united still...I believe that those years were a fitting and acceptable preparation for God's school."[100]

When asked what would be a lasting tribute at the school, Grace suggested a sundial be placed "in some spot on campus known as Sunshine Corner." Her son loved the "out of doors, the trees, the birds, the sunshine and the rain."[101]

After the service at Plymouth, Col. John C. Coolidge traveled to the capital with his son. Frank Stearns and his wife had accompanied the Coolidges throughout the long ordeal and were there as well. The Coolidges dug up a spruce tree from Plymouth to plant on the south grounds in memory of Calvin Jr.[102] After his grandfather left, plans for John were changed. He was not to attend military training at Camp Devens. He was needed to comfort his mother. One day he was the only guest on the *Mayflower* as it lifted anchor for a sail! Mrs. Coolidge urged the president to return to Plymouth "to be near for a little while the last resting place of her beloved son."[103] During the summer and autumn of 1924, about 500 people a day visited the very remote grave of their son in Plymouth.[104] Grace sent flowers three times a week.

---

[99] Grace Coolidge to Mrs. Irvine, August 25, 1924, Mercersburg Academy archives.
[100] Grace Coolidge to Mrs. Irvine, June 4, 1925, Mercersburg Academy archives.
[101] Grace Coolidge to Dr. Irvine, September 27, 1924, Mercersburg Academy archives.
[102] Ross, p. 123.
[103] Hall, p. 56.
[104] *Mercersburg Alumni Quarterly*, p. 57.

1924 CAMPAIGN

"Sustained by the great outpouring of sympathy from all over the nation, my wife and I bowed to the Supreme Will and with such courage as we had went on in the discharge of our duties," wrote Calvin Coolidge about this time after the death of their son.[105] Before they left the capital for their visit to Vermont, the president was to accept his party's nomination for another term. A "notable audience" gathered in Memorial Continental Hall to hear him on August 14, 1924. Grace wore all white and "was given an ovation when she appeared in her box, and bowed graciously in response."[106] Secretary of State Charles Evans Hughes led a rousing set of three cheers for the newly nominated president. After a train trip to Vermont, the Coolidges visited their son's grave as often as possible, but politics followed them to the homestead. Henry Ford, Harvey Firestone, and Thomas Edison dropped by on August 19th on a vacation diversion. Coolidge had supported selling the government facilities at Muscle Shoals to private industry and even though this did not work out, Ford endorsed the president in December of 1923. Ford was popular in the nation and his public support of the president was important.

What was unusual about this visit was the role of First Lady Grace Coolidge. Since they were away from the formality of the White House with their divided functions as president and first lady, she was up front and center in discussions with these important guests. She really seemed to come into her own. She had gained a new confidence during her 12 months as a first lady. "The conversation with Edison, Ford, and Firestone took a wide range, from reparations to diet" and sleep patterns.[107] Perhaps her husband's sorrow forced her to try even harder to relate to people to help him and his desire to serve a term as president in his own right. General Charles Dawes, the Vice Presidential nominee, visited the Coolidges on August 26th. He had just come from Maine where he denounced the Ku Klux Klan with a Klan official on the same podium. Coolidge pronounced the speech "good."[108] Grace felt very comfortable with General and Mrs. Dawes for they had all lived at the New Willard Hotel at the same time during the Coolidges' Vice Presidential years. "The friendship which developed outlasted the

---

[105] Coolidge, *The Autobiography of Calvin Coolidge*, p. 191.
[106] Hall, p. 57.
[107] Ross, p. 132.
[108] Bascom N. Timmons, *Charles G. Dawes, Portrait of an American* (New York: Henry Holt and Company, 1953) p. 235.

differences of opinion which sometimes resulted from expediency in matters of state."[109]

People in Plymouth often commented that elevation to the White House had not changed Grace, but the death of "their son had affected both the Coolidges deeply and had left them apathetic about the campaign."[110] The couple held a "neighbors' day" at Plymouth and greeted folks from near and far just as they had the day after the homestead inaugural of 1923. Photographers snapped away at each opportunity and that was one way of reminding people that there still was a presidential campaign on.

Sap Bucket Signing: Harvey Firestone, Calvin Coolidge, Henry Ford, Russell Firestone, Thomas Edison, Grace Coolidge and Col. John Coolidge, 1924

Grace had her walks to Calvin Jr.'s grave each day, down the road from the village, across the road around Plymouth Notch, and up to the cemetery, about one half a mile. She wanted to set up the weathervane Calvin Jr. had made for the garden across the street from the homestead. It was taken down for the winter, but Grace "found the nails and fixed it herself."[111]

---

[109] Grace Coolidge, *Good Housekeeping Magazine*, March, 1935 (New York: William Randolph Hearst)
[110] Ross, p. 129.
[111] Ross, p. 133.

On their return to Washington, the lingering thoughts of their lost son and their official mourning hovered over them. The president wanted to stay at the capital considering his job more important than campaigning.[112] He decided to stay off the campaign trail and stick to presidential duties. Grace immediately returned to entertaining. The Prince of Wales came to lunch with the Coolidge family including young John who had stayed on with his family for the summer. Grace enjoyed the prince. "He has a beautiful smile and has a way of winning your liking at once," she wrote to a friend.[113] The campaign season was still in full swing, and the Coolidges did travel for important, non-political speeches which were often broadcast on the radio. They went to Baltimore and to Philadelphia for the 150th anniversary of the meeting of the First Continental Congress. More importantly, Grace Coolidge found a diversion from all that had happened.

She found baseball! They went to many games and she loved it when her husband threw out the first ball of the season. In 1924 the World Series featured the Washington Senators against the New York Giants with many games played in the capital. During the first game, the president stood up to leave when the game was tied in the ninth inning. "Grace Coolidge sputtered, "Where do you think you're going? You sit down," as she grabbed his coat tails. The chief executive sat right back down."[114] He also stayed on for the 12 innings of their seventh game victory. Grace listened to games on the White House radio, and on October 10th she was the one to receive the managers of the two teams in the World Series at the White House. She also checked in the telegraph room for scores. "She used to come to games and sit right by the Senators' dugout. She came to the games with Cal and stayed there when the President would leave early. And then she'd come to other games alone. All the Washington players knew her and spoke to her. She was the most rabid baseball fan I ever knew in the White House," recalled Bucky Harris, the Senator's manager.[115]

After giving a speech, Calvin Coolidge's last words over the radio before the election on Tuesday, November 4th were, "To my father, who is listening in at my old home in Vermont, and to my other invisible audience I say good night."[116] These few words on this modern medium were moving to many people and Calvin Coolidge won the presidency in his own right in a landslide. Grace Coolidge had really been part of the equation despite her lack of involvement in

---

[112] Hall, p. 61.
[113] Grace Coolidge to Teresa Hills, August 23, 1924, Forbes Library.
[114] David Pietrusza, "Grace Coolidge—The First Lady of Baseball," *The Real Calvin Coolidge #10*, p. 24.
[115] Ibid, p. 25.
[116] Hall, p. 69.

public policy. Her management of the White House, their social life, the official life, and their small family was important for this candidate. "The voters respected the purity of his private life, his simplicity, his freedom from sham and pretense" according to biographer Claude M. Fuess.[117] "One flag, one country, one conscience, one wife, and never more than three words will do him all his life," summed up another biographer William Allen White.[118]

Now that Calvin Coolidge had won his own term as president, he would be formally sworn in as president in Washington D.C. with his family and friends in attendance. In photographs of the first couple, in an open car on the way to the inauguration, she is the radiant one. Her husband is unsmiling. First Lady Grace Coolidge wore "an ensemble dress of gray, gray shoes and stockings, and a gray hat with a plume of burnt goose."[119] All eyes would be on this glamourous figure. Son John, all of 19 years old, had left his college, Amherst, to attend with grandfather Col. John Coolidge of Plymouth and grandmother Mrs. Andrew I. Goodhue of Northampton. At the end of the ceremony they drove up Pennsylvania Avenue "amid a warmly cheering crowd."[120] After lunch a military parade drove by the White House with an artillery battalion and thirty-two tanks. As their racket shook the gates, "Mrs. Coolidge laughingly put her hands to her ears as though to shut out the din."[121] When the first woman governor passed the reviewing stand, Grace gave a warm greeting. The Daweses attended the charity ball, but the Coolidges dined with guests at the White House. The president greeted members of the Massachusetts legislature at the Cairo Hotel. Then Calvin returned to the White House by 9:30 p.m. to turn in for the evening. They were not the life of the party. Too much had happened. The president's voice was strained; he mainly spent time with old associates. Grace did not lead any dances as she had when he became governor. She stayed with her husband for a quiet ending to the day.

After the election, one reporter for the *Evening Star*, Sallie V.H. Pickett, wrote of her impressions of First Lady Grace Coolidge noting that "her personality" was "her strongest point" "and she brought to the White House a spontaneous atmosphere, a big joyousness which it had not known since the day President Cleveland took his bride there as the First Lady of the Land."[122] Grace was 45 years old, "possessed of poise, graciousness to a marked degree, a keen,

---

[117] Ross, p. 139.
[118] Ibid.
[119] Jerry Wallace, "Calvin Coolidge's Third Oath: Washington, March 4, 1925, the Seventy-Fifth Anniversary," *The Real Calvin Coolidge #16*, p. 31.
[120] Ibid, p. 37.
[121] Ibid, p. 39.

intelligent understanding of those around her, teeming with vitality, gently sympathetic, industrious, painstaking, meticulously neat, fond of music, fond of children and flowers and everything that makes the world lovelier—that is Mrs. Coolidge."[123] There was more comment in the press of how different the presidential couple appeared to the public. "Where Calvin Coolidge is a man of few words, Grace Goodhue Coolidge is a delightful conversationalist; where he has a dry sort of humor, she bubbles over with fun and good nature, where he is almost embarrassed at social functions, she is at ease."[124] "Mrs. Coolidge is a type that would attract attention in almost any group of women. She is of medium height with dark eyes, and dark hair, just beginning to be tinged with grey."[125]

Grace had become very competent in handling social relations. Calvin relied on Grace to invite the right people.[126] She knew what his priorities were now. As the president, he began his second term taking strong positions about a few issues. Many were popular and of course this was one reason the public welcomed the Coolidges with such affection wherever they went. He urged the country to join the World Court for international "concord and peace."[127] Congress approved the Court protocols with five reservations in January of 1926. Since the Court and League would not accept one reservation, it was stalled and Coolidge suspended this initiative. Domestically, he was opposed to fixing the price of farm products and was for protective tariffs. He felt strongly about tax reduction and allowing states a "greater degree of authority in their own local affairs."[128]

The presidential couple was quite popular in the country. In October of 1925, when they traveled to Omaha, Nebraska for a convention of the American Legion, crowds came to see them when their train stopped. 3000 people met them in Flora, Illinois. At the gathering, a cry of "Mrs. Coolidge" went up as she received a bouquet of orchids. They traveled to Chicago for the convention of American Farm Bureau Federation members. Wives of the farmers hosted a luncheon for Mrs. Coolidge. "Mrs. Coolidge's million dollar smile…is a great political asset" and "It is known to Americans everywhere that Mrs. Coolidge does most of the smiling for the Coolidge family…"[129]

---

[122] Hall, p. 71.
[123] Ibid.
[124] Hall, p. 95.
[125] Hall, p. 96.
[126] *The Autobiography of Calvin Coolidge*, p. 206.
[127] Lathem, p. 216.
[128] Lathem, p. 217.
[129] Hall, p. 179.

PETS AND HOBBIES

Grace and Calvin each had their own menagerie of pets, and then also shared them with each other. Pets were part of their household from the start, but at the White House with so many people wanting to shower them with gifts, giving them pets was popular. One time Grace Coolidge typed a list with the name of each animal and a description of their personality. She did not even write what kind of animal they were in most instances. "Pets of the White House: Tiger: The Wanderer [cat], Blacky: The Mighty Hunter [cat], Peter Pan: The Rascal [wire haired fox terrier], Rob Roy: The Wise [white collie], Paul Pry: The Guardian [Airedale], Beans: The Interloper [Boston Bulldog], Prudence Prim: The Flapper [white collie], Rebecca Raccoon: The Mischievous [raccoon], Tiny Tim: The Independent [chow dog], Calamity Jane: The Eccentric [white collie], Blackberry: The Willful [Black chow], Ruby Rough: The Foundling, King Cole: The Seeker [a black Belgian Gruenendahl], Bruno: the Bear, Wild Bill: The Wildcat, Princess Pat: The Peacock, Rubbery Rube: The Hippopotamus, Tax Reduction and Budget Bureau: Twin Lion cubs."[130] Starting with Bruno the animal type is described by Grace on her list.[131] Most interesting is Rebecca the raccoon who was sent as a contribution to the Thanksgiving feast; the animal loving couple rescued her to tame her into an "amiable, domesticated creature and interesting pet."[132] Grace even drew a picture for a treehouse with a wire fence built around it on the White House grounds for Rebecca. "She enjoyed nothing better than being placed in a bath tub with a little water in it and given a cake of soap with which to play," observed the first lady of the raccoon.[133] Since Rebecca looked lonely, they found her a companion named Reuben, but he escaped many times. Rebecca was eventually given to the zoo. Prudence Prim, the white collie, was brought in to be the companion to Rob Roy. She was Grace's guardian "never leaving my side when I was in the house, and sleeping by my bed or on my couch at night."[134] Both Calvin and Grace enjoyed playing with the animals where they could relax and show them affection. Grace wrote, "I am unable to understand how anyone can get along without some sort of pet."[135]

---

[130] Grace Coolidge, materials for *American Magazine*, Forbes Library collection,.
[131] Author added animal type.
[132] Grace Coolidge, materials for *American Magazine*, Forbes Library Collection, p. 12.
[133] Ibid.
[134] Ibid, p. 13.
[135] David Pietrusza, "Wombats and Such: Calvin and Grace Coolidge and Their Pets", *The Real Calvin Coolidge #14*, p.25.

Grace loved the gardens at the White House. Her first housekeeper compared her favorably to Mrs. Taft and the first Mrs. Wilson as being far more of a gardener than they were.[136] She added a Vermont birch tree and a water-lily pond to the grounds.[137] She seemed to open all the garden shows in the city.

She was also an amateur photographer. Her home movies were shown on the train as the Coolidges returned from Kansas City in November of 1926 where they dedicated the World War I Memorial.[138]

First Lady Grace Coolidge and her pet raccoon, Easter egg rolling, 1925 (Courtesy Library of Congress through the Vermont Historical Society)

---

[136] Jaffray, p. 117.
[137] Ross, p. 114.
[138] Hall, p. 186.

Grace liked to keep her hands busy. She knitted and crocheted as much as possible, often when listening to ball games on the radio.

WHITE HOUSE AS MUSEUM AND HISTORIC SITE

Grace Coolidge came to the White House and expected to see a museum; a place where furniture and paintings reflected prior administrations and the history of the establishment. She was "disappointed" to see "so little of the original furniture there."[139] Her kinsman had sailed in the Franklin Exploration of 1845 and an oak disk made from the timbers of the ship was presented by Queen Victoria to America "in appreciation of the American expedition sent to attempt to rescue them."[140] She was able to locate the disk in the President's study.

Under her instructions, the old cabinet table used for the treaty of peace with Spain was carried down to the east room for the signing of another peace treaty, the Kellogg Briand Pact of 1929.[141] Grace used the Lincoln bedroom, and had a bed made for the Lincolns installed there. She crocheted a coverlet for this bed and hoped that "each mistress of the President's house will leave there some token which shall go down through the ages."[142]

To gather historical pieces of furniture, a joint resolution was passed by Congress at Grace's request authorizing the "acceptance of such gifts as people might be induced to make towards this end."[143] The Green Parlor was refurbished under this plan. "This was the first legal recognition that the President's house also functioned as a museum."[144] She also received $50,000, up from the annual $20,000 to redecorate. She appointed experts to an advisory committee to guide her, the first ever established for the White House. She wanted to furnish the family quarters in a "colonial" style. She requested the family quarters be painted and plastered in 1925 and would consult with her committee "only about furnishings."[145]

A few of the esteemed committee members met and were "piqued that they had not been consulted."[146] The American Institute of Architects turned to

---

[139] *Grace Coolidge: An Autobiography*, p. 81.
[140] Ibid, p.1.
[141] Ibid, p. 82.
[142] Ibid, p. 83.
[143] Ibid, p. 84.
[144] Seale, p. 864.
[145] Ibid, p. 866.
[146] Ibid.

Theodore Roosevelt's letter of 1908 where they were to keep "a perpetual eye of guardianship over the White House."[147] Grace's committee of experts and the A.I.A. were in a battle to supervise this White House restoration. The committee accepted a donation by Harold I. Pratt to decorate the Green Room, part of the public space at the White House. *The Literary Digest* even polled their readers about a choice of White House style and most wanted American colonial.[148]

Newspapers picked up the controversy in the summer of 1925 and President Coolidge felt forced to take action. "There would be no refurnishing," said the President.[149] What he meant was that the public rooms, Red and Green, would only have repainting. The family quarters were to be done over without public comment or committees. For Grace, this was an example of a committee of the high and mighty getting ahead of itself. She had not given them proper oversight and now their plans were cancelled to prevent further embarrassment to her husband.

The structural condition of the White House did have to be addressed, however. The roof and attic had to be replaced according to Colonel Sherrill, director of parks and grounds. The family would need to move while work took place. Congress granted $375,000 for rebuilding the attic and roof and the ceilings of the second floor.[150] The new head of parks and grounds, U.S. Grant III, hired a member of the original committee, William Adams Delano, a New York architect, to redesign the third floor. The family was to move for 125 days in March of 1927 to 15 Dupont Circle, the Patterson mansion. Grace packed up their luggage, pets, and personal possessions; then her husband was driven over on March 2. One morning, during construction, Grace donned a construction hard hat and inspected the goings on and was so thankful that workmen spent nights and weekends there to get the work done on time. Grace did make her mark on this design. She wanted a "sky parlor" which was built on the roof of the south portico and hidden from view by a stone balustrade.[151] It offered views of the Washington Monument and the Mall as well as sunshine and fresh air. It also was a retreat for the family where the prying eyes of staff and the world could be avoided.

Since approximately $53,000 had been saved from the renovation project, the advisory committee revived itself but was heavily directed by Col. U.S. Grant III and Mrs. Coolidge. Grace sorted through the attic for historic pieces before spending any more money. Then the committee led by Mrs. Harriet Pratt brought

---

[147] Ibid.
[148] Ibid, p. 868.
[149] Ibid.
[150] Ibid, p.874.
[151] Ibid., p. 877.

in furnishings from the Federalist era. As the Coolidge term ended, Mrs. Pratt complained that a "supervising committee" from the Smithsonian museum would have had more power and influence. She was criticizing Grace who "turned her interests elsewhere."[152] The first lady had become accustomed to doing the next thing and looking forward to the next project. She had done all she could to restore history and dignity to the White House as a museum.

ADVOCACY

Grace Coolidge had been an advocate for those who had physical handicaps or economic deprivation for as long as she could remember. She had seen the needs of deaf children at a very young age. Now she had the opportunity to highlight those needs and gain more resources for groups that had formed to assist the disadvantaged of society. She publicly enrolled her husband as a member of the American Red Cross in 1925. (He was the President of the organization as well, since they were the ones to respond to national emergencies.) She was a sponsor of the annual Christmas Seal campaign of the National Tuberculosis Association, lighting candles for its opening.[153] She helped begin a drive in Washington for the Young Women's Christian Association's new building. She made regular visits to the Walter Reed hospital to visit veterans and visited the Children's hospital on holidays. Their dogs, Rob Roy and Prudence Prim, were often on these trips to cheer up the service men. She gave out baskets at the Salvation Army and greeted over 1000 youngsters from the Central Union Mission for Christmas. She launched numerous projects in Washington such as the Washington City Orphan asylum building.

Her most ambitious project was the fund drive for the Clarke School for the Deaf in Northampton, Massachusetts. Clarence W. Barron had begun the fund raising drive in 1927 and the Coolidges lent their names to the drive. Two million dollars was to be raised and the president wrote a letter of approval including, "It is my hope that this foundation may result now only in broadening the sphere of usefulness of Clarke School, but may also help to arouse a greater interest in the problems of the deaf and in this humanitarian work which has so seemingly failed to keep pace with progress in other fields."[154]

---

[152] Ibid, p. 883.
[153] Hall, p. 138.
[154] Ibid, p. 302.

Grace kept up an active communication with her fraternity when they were creating the Settlement School, the first philanthropic project of any women's fraternity, in Gatlinburg, Tennessee to educate mountain children in one of the poorest areas of the country. In 1924, two teachers taught 89 pupils in a one room school building. A health center was added as was a junior high school, industrial high school and scholarships. In 1928, a high school was built with the Grace Coolidge Library of some 3,500 volumes. Students could even board at the school.[155] Basketmaking as an industry was begun there in 1915, and weaving in 1920. One of the highlights of the visit to Kansas City by the Coolidges for the Liberty Memorial Dedication in November of 1926, was the presentation by her fraternity of wool fabric woven at the Settlement School by a 16-year old "mountain girl."[156]

Also in 1926, one of their first visitors was Helen Keller, the blind and deaf disability leader. Helen Keller read lips with her hands and was photographed with each of the presidential couple "reading them" with her hands. The president was described by Miss Keller as "sweet water after a thaw" by which she must have meant that having a presidential couple interested in the work of the blind was refreshing.[157]

Advocating the arts was so important to this First Lady. She drew attention to the arts by attending musical and theatrical shows continually during their years at the White House. This was always written up in the newspapers across the country. "Mrs. Coolidge's genuine love of music has been one of the outstanding features of her regime as First Lady. Seldom is there a notable concert without Mrs. Coolidge occupying the presidential box."[158]

FAMILY

Both Coolidges were very busy in their jobs in Washington and usually only traveled for business. Yet their family members were so important to them. The President checked on his father as much as he could. He was frustrated that his father would not install a telephone to make his communication easier. His father was the one he always wanted to impress and whose respect he hoped to gain. In 1925, Frank Stearns convinced the presidential couple to hold the Summer White

---

[155] Pi Beta Phi Archives, the history of the Settlement School.
[156] Jerry L. Wallace, "Calvin Coolidge and the Liberty Memorial", *The Real Calvin Coolidge,* #18, p. 54.
[157] Hall, p. 148.
[158] Ibid, p. 154.

House at White Court in Swampscott, Massachusetts. The New England location gave them easy access to a short car ride to Plymouth, Vermont, home of Calvin's father. Son John was sent to his grandfather's to shingle his house and to construct a new chimney. This has all the markings of a presidential decision to keep the young man engaged in positive work since cameras were always trained on the eligible bachelor. On July 3, 1925, Calvin Coolidge wrote his father ending with "I send love on my birthday, Your son, Calvin Coolidge."[159] His 80 year old father had surgery for an abscess of the prostate gland by a Boston doctor sent by his son. When the president visited his father "thousands along the way" greeted him.[160] Very few fathers had lived to see their sons become president. "I am sure I came to it very largely by your bringing up and your example. If that was what you wanted you have much to be thankful for that you have lived to so great an age to see it," wrote the president on August 2, 1925.[161] He really wanted his father to join them at the White House for better medical care and a warmer climate.

Grace Coolidge loved the holidays; they were a time to decorate and enjoy the fun of life. Her husband thought of who was missing from the celebration: his sister, his mother, his step-mother and now his younger son. New inventions such as the telephone and the radio were used by the president to reach his father. Calvin's radio address in Chicago of 1925 was heard by him. Calvin even complained about being stuck in Washington where he could not see his father as much as he would have wished. "I suppose I am the most powerful man in the world but great power does not mean much except great limitations. I cannot have any freedom even to go and come. I am only in the clutch of forces that are greater than I am. Thousands are waiting to shake my hand today."[162] (The Washingtons had set this precedent of greeting the public on New Year's Day; now over 3,000 people came to shake hands with the president and first lady.)

Grace and Father Coolidge had a very special relationship. He told the press, "She has always been helpful to Cal and kind to us. He was fortunate in getting such a fine girl for a wife."[163] The couple did head for Vermont when his father's condition worsened, but he had passed away by the time they braved the snows to get there on March 19, 1926. When they reached Plymouth by sleigh, captured on newsreels of the time, only the funeral was to be arranged. As Calvin said, "It

---

[159] Lathem, p. 208.
[160] Ibid, p. 210.
[161] Ibid., p. 211.
[162] Ibid., p. 219
[163] Ross, p. 173.

costs a great deal to be President."[164] He turned even more to Grace after this loss. "For she was the sunshine and the joy in his life—his rest when tired—his solace in time of trouble. Deep, indeed, went the roots of Calvin Coolidge, and they were close bound about that wife of his, and the children."[165]

SON JOHN

Grace wanted to spend time with her son before he went off to college. John stayed at the White House that summer. Grace realized that John missed his brother when at the White House and really needed to be around other young people.[166] When John left Amherst briefly to travel to Washington for his father's inauguration in March of 1925, he learned that the governor of Connecticut was traveling on his same train with his family. John entered the car and paid his respect to the governor, his wife and two daughters. One daughter, Florence, attended Mt. Holyoke College, not far from Amherst College where John attended. John said he would give her a call after the inauguration, and this led to a series of dates. At White Court, the Summer White House, in 1925, John complained to Admiral Boone that he was not allowed to play tennis and "might as well be in a penitentiary as White Court."[167] In the summer of 1926 at White Pine Camp, Boone also observed son John snapping at his father. It seemed that the President, according to Frank Stearns, "did not understand" his son and differed with Grace as to how to deal with him.[168] Stearns felt John was "farmed out" too much and needed his mother's influence. Of course, John was probably the only one in the world disagreeing with his father, the President of the United States. His rebellion must have been a real shock especially after the father's experience with his other son who liked to joke and excel as much as possible. Grace felt that her husband reprimanded her son too much and drove him away.[169] Grace wrote her son every day to keep up communication. She was very torn in her devotions. She wrote of John to a friend, "I am awful sorry for him. He labors under difficult conditions."[170] If she challenged her husband on this, he would

---

[164] Lathem, p. 224.
[165] Ross, p.188 quoting Mary Randolph
[166] Grace Coolidge to Mrs. Maude Trumbull, April 10, 1927, The Calvin Coolidge Memorial Collection, #19.
[167] Admiral Joel T. Boone diary, the Library of Congress, July 31, 1925
[168] Ibid, August 11, 1926.
[169] Ibid, August 12, 1926.
[170] Grace Coolidge to Teresa Hills, October 12, 1926, Forbes Collection.

retaliate and not speak to her for 3 days.[171] This was typical of Calvin; he would give her the silent treatment if he disagreed with her. John did visit White Pine Camp where he continued to criticize his father. He was admonished with an interesting prospect. A member of the Secret Service would live with him at school that fall.

President Coolidge decided to send Col. Edmund W. Starling of the Secret Service, age 50, to room with John at his school. John's grades were not high enough, according to his father, and the temptations of the Jazz age were all around at an exclusive school. Grace had written to a friend, "his father would not approve of his leaving Amherst (for a visit). He thinks he should put in all of his time there. He just must pass this year."[172] Starling soon learned to "get lost" every Saturday night after they took a trolley ride to Mt. Holyoke College to see Miss Trumbull.[173] According to the president, John was to "set schedule for each day and then stick to it."[174] Starling was able to leave Amherst at Christmas but another agent was sent to replace him. John's progress at college was uneven and his father was not terribly impressed with his work there. Calvin and Grace were in Superior, Wisconsin in 1928 at their Summer White House when John graduated. Grace wrote her friend Teresa Hills that she was glad she had attended the commencement exercises and that the Stearnses were there. "His father and I gave him a ring which we sent to him by Mr. Stearns. He said he had it and couldn't thank us enough but he didn't say whether he had given it to Florence or not."[175]

John Coolidge had indeed proposed to Florence Trumbull! Governor and Mrs. Trumbull had visited the White House the previous April and the families were getting to know each other. The president took an instant liking to Florence, whom he nicknamed "Miss Connecticut", and things seemed to go better with his son as well. Finding a job for his son which did not take advantage of his father's fame was difficult. The president even wrote Governor Trumbull for help in the matter. A job at the New Haven Railroad was secured for John and thus the couple could announce their engagement. In May of 1929, Grace wrote her son about the impending marriage, "Not a word from father—I shall not mention it until he does."[176] "I cannot fully express myself until I can get hold of the two of

---

[171] Ibid, August 13, 1926.
[172] Grace Coolidge to Teresa Hills, November 1, 1927, Forbes Collection.
[173] Edmund W. Starling, p. 244.
[174] Ibid.
[175] Grace Coolidge to Teresa Hills, June 24, 1928, Forbes Library Collection
[176] Grace Coolidge to John Coolidge, May 15, 1929, The Calvin Coolidge Memorial Foundation Collection

you and squeeze you!" she exclaimed.[177] Now she really had two lovely young people to nurture and encourage. She was so pleased, and wrote,

> "John, you are a son for a mother to be proud of and I want you to always feel that I am standing by ready to do anything for you and Florence. You two together should make something very beautiful of your lives. Just don't let little things be-cloud your vision and when the rough places have to be gotten over hold your chin up, throw your shoulders back and go forward—for it's the rough places which steady the feet and strengthen the muscles—life is so beautiful—never do anything which will mar the sweetness of it. So shall each year bring you new appreciation of it."[178]

Calvin and Grace still had John on a very limited budget and his salary was small. To help him out, his wash was done each week at the White House and sent to him in Connecticut![179]

GRACE'S MOTHER

In her published articles, Grace Coolidge rarely discussed her mother, but in her letters to friends, her mother was a constant concern. Lemira Goodhue did not seem to play much of a role in the early years of Calvin's rise up the political ladder. Grace even wrote a friend that during the Vice Presidential years, her parents did not visit Washington since it was a wild and boisterous place when the Hardings ruled the White House. However, as the only offspring, Grace felt responsible for her mother after her father died and moved her mother to the two family house in Northampton in 1923. Of course, Lemira did attend the 1925 inauguration of Calvin Coolidge and did stay on at the White House for some time. One of her highlights was a trip on the *Mayflower*! Finally she must have approved of her daughter's choice for a husband!

Grace's friends and housekeeper Alice Reckahn looked after her mother in Northampton until December of 1927 when she was moved to a hospital. At one point, when Alice had to leave, Lemira had been sent to Burlington to board at Mrs. Stevens' house. John also stayed there when he attended the University of

---

[177] Ibid.
[178] Grace Coolidge to John Coolidge, June 19, 1929, The Calvin Coolidge Memorial Foundation Collection.
[179] John Coolidge to Grace Coolidge, November 9, 1928, The Calvin Coolidge Memorial Foundation Collection.

Vermont for a summer course in 1926.[180] Grandson John constantly looked in on his maternal grandmother when he was at nearby Amherst College, but after graduation, he lived in New Haven, Connecticut.

Grace credited her mother as teaching her about the "loving care of our heavenly Father" which sustained her to face the death of Calvin Jr. and wrote her friend, Hillsy, that her mother "really is a dear, in many ways."[181] "She is quite remarkable in the way she accepts everything that comes to her and fights her way through."[182] The first lady was to travel to Cuba in January of 1928, and was worried that she would be far away. Grace took advantage of having an Assistant White House physician who could travel to Massachusetts to check on the treatments her mother was receiving. Dr. Boone put "pep and interest into the physician in charge."[183] She kept her concern for her mother's health from her husband. "I have decided not to go into details with the President. He knows that mother has not been so well for the last ten days and that she is growing weaker. I think it is better that he should have the rest of his time here as free from extra care as may be. If he knew that I am anxious it would be less so. I cannot do mother any good."[184] Her mother had "an abdominal mass presumed to be malignant."[185] Grace, despite her own chronic fatigue, went with Dr. Boone on three trips to visit her mother in Northampton and her son at Amherst. When the Coolidges left for their Summer White House in 1928 in Wisconsin, Dr. Boone was to stay behind so he could visit Mrs. Goodhue should that be necessary.[186] Memory loss was another complication, noted in Grace's letters to friends. In 1928, Grace visited her mother on the way to touring the ravages of the flood in Vermont. Her mother was no longer able to recognize people and went "where human kindness cannot reach."[187] Mrs. Goodhue died on October 24, 1929.

FRIENDS

Family members were very important to Grace and Calvin Coolidge, but their relationship with Frank and Emily Stearns was central to their political rise and

---

[180] Grace Coolidge to Teresa Hills, June 6, 1926, Forbes Collection.
[181] Grace Coolidge to Admiral Boone, May 9, 1925 Library of Congress Collection and Grace Coolidge to Teresa Hills, October 14, 1923, Forbes Collection.
[182] Grace Coolidge to Teresa Hills, December 16, 1927, Forbes Collection
[183] Grace Coolidge to Admiral Boone, April 9, 1928, Library of Congress Collection
[184] Grace Coolidge to Admiral Boone, August 26, 1928, Library of Congress Collection
[185] Heller, p. 112.
[186] Heller, p. 115.
[187] Grace Coolidge to Teresa Hills, September 26, 1928, Forbes Collection

their lives in the White House as well. Lillian Rogers Parks, with her view from the backstairs at the White House, told her daughter, "Every First Family seems to have one couple upon whom it relies for true friendship. For the Coolidges, it was Mr. and Mrs. Frank W. Stearns of Boston, Massachusetts, owners of a large department store. They seemed to be at the White House half the time."[188] Frank Stearns was interviewed by the *Boston Globe*'s Louis M. Lyons when Calvin Coolidge won a term in his own right in 1924. Stearns had spent eight years devoting his energy and "his advertising genius to 'sell' his conviction about Calvin Coolidge to the people of America."[189] Calvin Coolidge was 17 years younger and almost a son to Stearns. With a "hunch" for sizing up men, Stearns thought that Coolidge "was the greatest man of his time, the man who was to lead the American Nation for the welfare of the world."[190] Stearns was instrumental in pushing Calvin Coolidge to be Lt. Governor, Governor, and a candidate for the Presidency in 1920. Then, when Calvin became the president in 1923, Stearns came to the White House as his best friend and "the President's eyes and ears."[191] He was the "liaison officer between the outside world and the White House."[192] He was often sent out on delicate missions for the president such as an offer of an ambassadorship to Frank O. Lowden.

Grace relied on Frank Stearns to learn more about her husband's political plans and she looked to Emily Stearns as one might look to a mother for guidance. Grace wrote that she should "pay tribute to one of the most beautiful friendships I have ever known" referring to Frank Stearns and that they often "put our heads together" to understand "presidential confidences."[193] When Stearns spoke of his nine grandchildren at dinner one evening, Grace corrected him and added in her two sons. Actually the boys did call Mrs. Stearns "Grandma Stearns." Grace called her "mother."[194] Grandma Stearns stayed with Grace for a month after the death of Calvin Jr. In turn when Mrs. Stearns was ill, she lived at the White House for weeks receiving care.[195] In June of 1928, Grace wrote Frank Stearns from Superior, Wisconsin about their time there and concluded, "Every day, I think of

---

[188] Parks, p.191.
[189] *The Boston Globe*, November 9, 1924, p. 6 in Amherst College Archives.
[190] Ibid.
[191] M.E. Hennessy, "Believed in Coolidge" in *Liberty Magazine*, October 15, 1924, Amherst College Archives, p. 61.
[192] Ibid.
[193] *Grace Coolidge:An Autobiography*, p. 86.
[194] *The Boston Globe*, op.cit.., p. 6.
[195] W.A. Gavin, *The Boston Herald*, February 9, 1929, Amherst College Archives.

how good you are to us and thank God for friends like you. With Love, Sincerely, Grace Coolidge."[196]

Grace Coolidge's friend from her days as a young mother on Massasoit Street in Northampton was Mrs. Reuben B. Hills or Hillsy. With Grace's political husband away so much in the early years and with no family car in Northampton, Grace and the boys were given rides by Mrs. Hills to market on a daily basis.[197] Thus they began a lifelong friendship. Hillsy was married to a local businessman and had one son, Jack. A highpoint for Mrs. Hills was a visit to the White House for the 1925 inauguration and dinner with the family and Mr. and Mrs. Stearns at the end of the day. On November 1, 1927, in a letter to Hillsy, Grace started to complain about life in the White House, "I guess nobody but you has a real idea of how shut in and hemmed about I feel. Well, I'm not complaining—I'm only telling you."[198] Grace had complained about her lack of privacy especially after having endured the death of her younger son in the public eye. Hillsy was to visit for a dinner and a musicale to cheer Grace.[199] In the winter of 1927-1928, Grace became seriously ill. "The public never learned how critical her condition was," wrote biographer Ross.[200] Calvin turned to Mrs. Hills and said, "Hillsy, I'm afraid that Mammy will die."[201] Hillsy stayed with Grace and read to her as they listened to the Victrola in the sky parlor. Dr. Boone characterized Grace's condition as "chronic fatigue" and then with further tests found an enlarged and misplaced right kidney.[202] Only during the summer of 1928 at Superior, Wisconsin did Mrs. Coolidge bounce back to her old self.

One outlet for Grace's opinions was the round robin letters where she wrote her true feelings to her fraternity sisters. From the time she became a member of the fraternity at the University of Vermont, she wanted to be part of their circle. In March of 1925, when she received an LL.D. from Boston University, she wrote of her experience and how she should really have received a D.D. "for a Doctor of Domesticity! The fleeting glimpse of about half of our little band was very tantalizing at the tea which followed that induction ceremonies but you who were there will never know how good you looked to me as you gathered in a little group on the balcony. My life now seems made of tantalizing glimpses. It is terrible to have to spread out so thin."[203]

---

[196] Grace Coolidge to Frank W. Stearns, June, 1928, Amherst College archives.
[197] Ross, p. 35.
[198] Grace Coolidge to Teresa Hills, Forbes Library.
[199] Grace Coolidge to Teresa Hills, Forbes Library.
[200] Ross, p. 238.
[201] Ibid.
[202] Heller, p. 112.
[203] Grace Coolidge to Phi Beta Phi sisters, March, 1925, Phi Beta Phi Fraternity archives.

Dr. Joel T. Boone, the assistant White House physician, became a friend and confidant. Grace turned to him initially for advice on where the boys should attend preparatory school, but since he was bored and had extra time in his secondary role at the White House, he took interest in the boys almost like an older brother. Their father did not play any sports with them, but Boone did. Grace turned to Boone for advice on medical matters just as the prior First Lady, Florence Harding had done. Grace asked him to extend his medical care to her mother, moved to Northampton after her father's death, and she invited his wife and daughter to activities at the White House. Suzanne Boone, his daughter, was special to Grace; the little girl was even invited to stay overnight at the White House and brought by the presidential couple to the circus![204] Boone, in his diary, often complained about the president, but when gazing on Mrs. Coolidge saw only "the disposition of an angel."[205] He characterized her as "gracious, loving, considerate, communicative and supportive person" who was so likable.[206]

FAMOUS VISITORS

Will Rogers called Grace Coolidge his "public female favorite no.1" and made her rather famous with discussion of her in his routines.[207] It is rare that a President gets special letters from a famous personality or gets a book dedicated to him, but in the case of Will Rogers this happened. Will Rogers had a radio show, wrote a daily newspaper column, and acted in movies. Rogers was really a modern star. He was "an astute and sagacious observer of politics and other foibles, a purveyor of great good humor, and a decent man who knew how to communicate decency masterfully.[208] He was a Democrat. *Letters of a Self-Made Diplomat to His President* was written in 1926 by Rogers and dedicated to three women: Mrs. Calvin Coolidge, Lady Nancy Astor, and Mrs. Alice Longworth. These women, according to Rogers, "have the keenest sense of humor that it has been my good fortune to encounter. They appreciate jokes even on their own husbands."[209] The humorous book was written on the premise that Rogers would represent the President on his trip to Europe. Of course, this was never arranged

---

[204] Milton F. Heller, Jr., "The Boones and the Coolidges," *The Real Calvln Coolidge* #14, p. 11.
[205] Ibid, p. 10.
[206] Ibid., P. 12.
[207] Ross, p. 191.
[208] Ben Yagod, *Will Rogers, A Biography* (New York: Alfred A. Knopf, 1993), p.xiii.
[209] Will Rogers, *Letters of a Self-Made Diplomat to His President* (New York: Albert and Charles Boni, 1926), p. 1.

except by "mental telepathy." The Coolidges did entertain Will Rogers on his return and Will commented on the president's wit, "He pulls 'em, if you don't get 'em, that's your fault."[210] He was also pleased to meet the first lady. "She is chuck plumb full of magnetism, and you feel right at home from the minute you get near her."[211] Grace also told Will Rogers that she "could do a much better imitation of her husband than Will could." He responded, "I believe it, but look what you had to go through to learn it."[212]

As Grace wrote, Lindbergh "has captured the love and admiration of the whole world, and held it."[213] Whereas the meeting with Will Rogers was a quiet one at the White House, the arrival of Charles A. Lindbergh after his solo nonstop flight in 33 and one half hours from New York to Paris in May of 1927 was rather dramatic. At the direction of the President, the aviator returned to America on board the USS Memphis. When the ship was sited in Washington DC, 50 pursuit planes and slower bombers were thick in the sky with the "dirigible *Los Angeles*"(christened by Grace) floating above.[214] Officers greeted Lindbergh and a car brought him through cheering mobs to the Washington Monument. Calvin Coolidge greeted him and his mother who had joined him for this moment. Coolidge gave an address to the country via radio and pinned the Distinguished Flying Cross on the young aviator. Then in March of 1928, Coolidge presented him with the Congressional Medal of Honor at the White House. "On the eve of his triumphal arrival back from Paris," his mother had dined with the Coolidges and Dwight Morrow, Ambassador to Mexico. When the Coolidges left for a meeting of the Bureau of the Budget, Mrs. Lindbergh and Mr. Morrow were left on their own. From that must have come the invitation to visit Mexico. When Lindbergh visited, he met Anne Morrow, his future wife.

SUMMER WHITE HOUSES

The White House staff wanted the presidential couple to leave during the summer so they could clean the White House.[215] If the family stayed there, this

---

[210] Ross, p. 192.
[211] Ibid., p. 194.
[212] Lance Brown, *On the Road with Will Rogers* (Brunswick, ME: Biddle Publishing Co., 1997), p. 21.
[213] *Grace Coolidge: An Autobiography*, p. 95.
[214] Walter S. Ross, *The Last Hero: Charles A. Lindbergh* (New York: Harper and Row, 1964) p.132.
[215] Jaffray, p. 127.

would need to be done "bit by bit, room by room."[216] Because so many visitors, about one thousand, came through the main floor of the Executive Mansion on a daily basis, the house needed an annual cleaning. In past summers, the Tafts had gone to Beverly Cove, Massachusetts and the Wilsons had gone to Cornish, New Hampshire. The Hardings kept the house open in the summer as did the Coolidges in 1924, except for a visit to Plymouth, Vermont. In 1925, the Stearnses leased a house next to theirs in Swampscott, Massachusetts, White Court, for the presidential family. Room for staff, secret service, physicians, servants, and chauffeurs was needed. A direct line by phone must be available. Silver and linen from the White House was packed up along with many of the pets. White Court provided two swimming pools and a beach which Grace used with the Secret Service keeping any curious person away. The president, however, could not find diversion or a good place to walk. Grace wrote her friend that she was now an "Indian maid" in color and strength.[217] Luckily the Presidential yacht *Mayflower* was in the harbor at Marblehead Neck so excursions could be arranged with parties of friends. The president refused to join the social swirl. They did not accept invitations from people in the area. Grace would have liked to spend another summer there near family and Massachusetts friends, but Calvin thought they should move "to get in touch with the people of different sections of the country insofar as possible."[218] Grace and Frank Stearns had been overruled.

White Pine Camp, 14 miles from Saranac Lake, New York, was chosen in 1926 for the Summer White House. Grace enjoyed swimming in a small lake and walking in the woods. Calvin's excellent fishing brought a special luncheon each day consisting of his catch. One of the cottages was made into the presidential office.

In 1927, the Black Hills of South Dakota was chosen with the Game Lodge in the State Game Preserve as their home. Eighty people left Washington for the Summer White House including office staff, servants, secret service, newspaper reporters and photographers. Executive offices were based at a high school in Rapid City. Grace enjoyed her "house by the side of a road" and wrote many letters sitting by the creek and watching goats, elk, and sheep up on the hillsides. The couple saw buffalo and visited "Indian reservations, and gold mines, attending rodeos and farmers' picnics."[219] The president was made a High Chieftain of the Sioux Nation and Mrs. Coolidge was given beaded moccasins. The president again took up fishing and presented many a delicious trout for the

---

[216] Ibid., p. 128.
[217] Grace Coolidge to Teresa Hills, August 7, 1925, Forbes Library Collection
[218] *Grace Coolidge: An Autobiography*, p. 91.
[219] Ibid., p. 95.

dinner table. The mountain stream was later named Grace Coolidge Creek.[220] John Coolidge arrived after his summer school at the University of Vermont and joined them for a visit to the Pine Ridge Indian Reservation.[221] The president seemed quite thrilled with the visit. He was given a saddle horse and two sheep! The newspaper reported that Mrs. Coolidge "had a smile for everybody and she won the hearts of us all."[222] Women's organizations sought her out for dedications and to give her presents. Both the president's birthday on July 4th and John's on September 7th were celebrated there.

August 2, 1927 was the fourth anniversary of Coolidge's succession to the presidency. Coolidge told Everett Sanders, his secretary, "If I should serve as president again, I should serve almost ten years, which is too long for a president in this country."[223] The president wanted to give the Republican party ample time to find someone else.[224] When Calvin left for the office that morning, he said, "I have been President for four years today."[225] Then he proceeded to hand reporters slips of paper with "I do not choose to run for President in 1928" typed on them. When Senator Arthur Capper sat down for lunch with Mrs. Coolidge and a Congressman, she did not comment on the announcement. Only after he asked her about it did she reply, "Isn't that just like the man! He never gave me the slightest intimation of his intention. I had no idea!"[226] However, she had been very much part of her husband's decision not to run again. On March 10th she had written her Northampton friend, "…the President has lots of fun telling me that I will soon be walking, riding in street cars and taxicabs. No terrors lie therein for me. I am keeping my walking apparatus in good trim."[227] Part of the reason why they were leaving was due to Grace. She did not really want to serve in her unelected office another four years. The President did not want to have her continue to carry this heavy responsibility.[228] Grace also crocheted a cover for the Lincoln bed with the years 1923-1929! She was counting on leaving.

Even though her husband was not running for office again, he chose to hold his Summer White House in Wisconsin in 1928. Trout fishing on the Brule River was the attraction! Cedar Island Lodge was found by Senator Irvine L. Lenroot for the presidential entourage. As 200 people in Washington packed up for the trip,

---

[220] *The Black Hills Engineer*, Vol XV, No.4, Rapid City, SD, p. 218.
[221] Ibid, p. 234.
[222] Ibid, p. 242.
[223] Sobel, p. 368.
[224] Ibid, p. 372.
[225] Ross, p. 221.
[226] Ross, p. 222.
[227] Grace Coolidge to Teresa Hills, March 10, 1927, Forbes Library.
[228] Fuess, p. 397.

Grace tried to revive herself from a bout with kidney trouble. To see the arrival of the presidential party, over 20,000 people surrounded the train depot. On July 1st, John arrived after graduating from college. The eight room bungalow, dining hall, greenhouse, stables, servant's quarters, power house, boat house, fish hatchery and other buildings in a park of 5000 acres of pine and cedar trees had streams winding all through it. Grace wrote Dr. Boone of her visit, "Life flows peacefully on here by the Brule. The days slip by and are gone before there is time to realize it and in almost no time at all we shall all be back in Washington, going down the home stretch. This has been the most quiet summer we have had, not so many guests. At times I have felt a bit desperate but not actively so. The Ringling Circus comes to Duluth on Thursday."[229] "This is a grand and glorious Fourth and the President's birthday," Grace wrote, "He staged some stuff for the photographers, this morning—went fishing, catching two fish at once; one on each fly—cut his birthday cake and passed it around and also cigars."[230] Obviously she and the president were enjoying the last months of the presidency. She also had seen the changes now with a lame-duck administration. "Yes," she wrote Hillsy, "it is wonderful to think that in a few months now the light of publicity will be elsewhere. And ever from now on it will be centered elsewhere. It is a wonderful service to render and after all six and a half years are a small portion of one's life."[231] "After being in the thick of it for so long I am thoroughly enjoying the side lines," she wrote when the Hoovers were to visit.[232] She walked four miles a day and swam in the glassed in pool. She was feeling much better, she confided to Hillsy.

On March 2,1929, Grace wrote Hillsy, "All set—facing North." She commented about a positive editorial her friend sent her as "very nice" but "please treat me rough when I get home and kick me about a bit so I'll realize that I'm human."[233]

What about these White House years as First Lady? Grace wrote her friend in January of 1929 about Lou Hoover coming in to take over her position. "I tell you it is pretty nice to have someone coming in whom you know and like and I am thinking how much easier it is for Mrs. Hoover who has lived in Washington so long and knows everybody than for a stranger." Then she continued, "There are so many currents and cross-currents that it seems to me it is easier to get along with

---

[229] Grace Coolidge to Dr. Boone, August 14, 1928, Library of Congress Collection.
[230] Grace Coolidge to Teresa Hills, July 5, 1928, Forbes Library.
[231] Grace Coolidge to Teresa Hills, June 24, 1928, Forbes Library.
[232] Ibid, July 12, 1928.
[233] Grace Coolidge to Teresa Hills, March 2, 1929, Forbes Library.

as few as possible."²³⁴ As she was leaving, Grace had the opinion that it was easier for the wife of a Senator as Florence Harding had been or the wife of a Commerce Secretary as Lou Hoover was. Grace had kept the job very non-political. She did not have a black book of people she did not like as Florence Harding had created. She tried to get along with everybody and that could be a strain at times.

To assess how successful she was as first lady, one should look at the various roles she mastered. As the wife of the head of state and head of the government, she became the social hostess par excellence. She had the clothes, looks, reputation and personality to charm everyone—royalty to White House staff. She kept up a demanding travel and public appearance schedule. She balanced "social affairs fit for dignitaries from the courts of Europe with the need to appease the popular taste for democratic simplicity."²³⁵ Social events enhanced the president's image and they brought leading figures of the political scene together. Pictures in newspapers at Summer White Houses show the First Lady talking with the movers and shakers of American life. Movie stars came to the White House to campaign for her husband!

She was comforting and nurturing to her partner, her husband, the president. Yet she was not a presidential partner since she did not get involved in politics. In addition, her management of the White House menus and staff was often overruled by her husband. With a change in housekeepers in 1926, she had more control over the budget and her husband was pleased with the arrangements.

Her interest in culture and antiques made her a preservationist of the White House. She was actively involved in renovation and restoration. She had asked for Congressional authority to accept antiques. Her only faux pas was her failure to strongly lead her collection committee. She promoted culture by showcasing the arts at the White House. She continued the White House musicales and looked for artists to play at the White House to entertain government leaders and international figures.

Grace restored dignity and family values to the White House after the Hardings flaunted the looser mores of the time. A church going, straight laced New England couple who obeyed Prohibition came into the White House after the death of Warren Harding. No more card playing, no more show girls, no more wild travels with the Ohio gang. No more political scandals. Traditional holidays were important to Grace and they reinforced religious holidays. Egg rolling for

---

²³⁴ Ibid, January 7, 1929
²³⁵ Robert P. Watson, "Nation's Social Hostess," *American First Ladies* (Hackensack, NJ: Salem Press, Inc., 2002) p. 349.

children was arranged on the White House grounds for Easter. Christmas carols were sung on the portico.

Following the example of Florence Harding and other First Ladies, Grace highlighted the needs of the ill and disabled in society. She brought her sunny disposition to the hospitals of recovering soldiers from World War I and to the needy children of the capitol. She kept up her interest in deaf education and helped lead a drive for increased funding for it. She was the one who enlisted her husband into supporting her cause— deaf children.

Family and friends sustained Grace Coolidge. From her earliest days as an only child, she had reached out for love and attention and had found it. She had raised two wonderful sons with minimal involvement from her husband. She was sorely tested by the death of their younger son. Her writings, her son's school, and her faith kept her strong to finish the term her husband won right after their son's death. Her joy in John's romance and engagement gave her a new family to nurture. As they left the White House, a wedding was to be planned for the same year, 1929. Grace always looked ahead.

Chapter 7

RETIREMENT FROM PUBLIC LIFE AND DEATH OF THE 30TH PRESIDENT

"As we turned and reentered the car I suddenly realized that I had come back to myself, that my husband was no longer the head of our great nation, and that he and I were free to come and go and order our lives according to the dictates of our hearts, responsible only to ourselves for the outcome of our decisions. Gone were the men of the Secret Service, the aides, the valet, the maid, and we were homeward bound," wrote Grace about the end of their term.[1]

Planning to leave the White House and return to their two family house in Northampton must have been very frustrating for Grace Coolidge. Here she was with gifts of state numbering in the hundreds (you were allowed to keep them in those days) and so little storage or living space. It was her job to move the family out of the White House and into 21 Massasoit Street, a house with seven rooms. This was bittersweet since she was leaving her surroundings and staff to function quite on her own, but would be reunited with friends dating back to their early days of marriage. Also, the couple was retired from official obligations after years of political appearances.

"I think I realized for the first time that I was really going when I looked up from the car and saw you at the window," Grace wrote about the drive to the station and looking up at Ellen Riley, still in her position as housekeeper at the White House.[2] Following Herbert Hoover's swearing in, the Coolidges' staff and friends gathered at Union Station in Washington to see them off to Northampton. Since Miss Jordan, a staff member, had tears streaming down her face, Grace

---

[1] *Grace Coolidge: An Autobiography*, p. 102-103.
[2] Grace Coolidge to Ellen Riley, March 6, 1929, Riley Papers.

wrote later, "I wanted to get off the train and grab her."[3] Their arrival in Northampton was heart warming. "It looked as though the whole town was out. Smith students were lined up in the road...Clarke School turned out in force...the newsgatherers and photographers were all over the place..."[4] Her husband remarked, "And this is private life!"[5]

Once they did arrive at 21 Massasoit Street, they were "buried deep in trunks, suitcases, boxes, barrels and crates but are gradually extricating ourselves," she wrote her former housekeeper.[6] Grace had sent a moving van ahead and even shipped things to her good friends for safe keeping. Grace was rather jovial in the letters to her former housekeeper, but their side of the two family house was crowded with not even a seat for visitors. The animals found it tight quarters as well. The well known joke about Calvin Coolidge was that he sat rocking on his chair on the porch of the two family house and people kept staring at him. Once when he heard a passerby say something uncomplimentary about his small house, the former President muttered "Democrats" under his breath. "The whole house...could be fitted into the state dining room of the Executive Mansion with room to spare," Grace wrote.[7] Housekeeper Alice Reckahn had stayed at the two family house to care for Mrs. Goodhue and was still there for the family's return.

Early in 1929, the couple traveled down to Florida and from there on to New Orleans to Hollywood! Grace wrote her Pi Beta Phi friends that five weeks in Florida were rather quiet. In New Orleans her husband "was tamed" with the atmosphere. She was impressed with the Hearst castle in California where they lived "like the knights and ladies of old" with modern "sound motion pictures" every night, being sent from Los Angeles by plane.[8]

They were surprised that the public and newspaper reporters still saw them as newsworthy. They thought they were out of the spotlight but somehow were still of interest. They were the first presidential couple, in the 1920s, to be photographed widely and seen in newsreels. Their Summer White Houses had been front page news. Every movement of their son John was watched!

There was another big publicity event of the year. It was a wonderful family affair: the wedding of John to Florence Trumbull, the daughter of the Governor of Connecticut, John H. Trumbull. Grace was overcome with joy from the start of this relationship. John was also very pleased that Governor Trumbull had taken

---

[3] Ibid.
[4] Ibid.
[5] Ibid.
[6] Grace Coolidge to Ellen Riley, March 15, 1929, Riley Papers.
[7] Ross, p. 259.
[8] Grace Coolidge to Round Robins, March 10, 1929, Pi Beta Phi Archives.

such an interest in him. John wrote his mother about the governor, his future father-in-law, "He's always wanted a son of his own, and I'm the nearest to it. He's certainly a peach."[9] The governor appointed John as a special aide with the rank of captain. John wanted to be on a governor's staff as his grandfather had once been on the staff of Governor William W. Stickney of Vermont. "It will make me pretty proud to tell my children that I was a captain on Governor Trumbull's staff when I was 22..."[10] Obviously he was getting respect and appreciation from his future father-in-law. His own father was so worried about his behavior and really tried to find him a job which would not bring public criticism of favoritism. Yet John still had great hopes for a better relationship with his father. He wrote his mother, "I'll be so glad when you and father get back home. Then everything will seem natural again, and I can see more of you."[11]

In May of 1929, Grace wrote her son, "I cannot fully express myself until I can get hold of the two of you and squeeze you!"[12] On Monday, September 23, 1929, the Plainville Congregational Church in Plainville, Connecticut was the scene for the wedding of the year! About 2,000 gawkers were there as witnesses to the comings and goings. The reception was at the Trumbull's home in Plainville with the Eddie Wittstein orchestra the couple had heard years before at a Sophomore Hop at Amherst College.[13] John's best man and two of their ushers were from a group of boys who had played together since early childhood and the minister had known John since he was 14.[14] Grace began an active correspondence with John's mother-in-law, Maude Trumbull. She gushed to her in one letter after the wedding, "…everytime I think of them a little warm glow of happiness comes stealing over me."[15] The two set up an apartment in New Haven, Connecticut and Grace, with her savings, gave them their bedroom furniture.

Just when her personal life was going well, Grace's mother took a turn for the worse. Grace wrote Dr. Boone that Mrs. Goodhue "seemed to balance on the verge of Eternity" at the hospital.[16] Lemira died about a month after John and Florence's wedding. This had been a long siege with Grace often leaving the White House to visit her mother in the hospital, and even arranging for Dr. Boone to make visits to her bedside. In the end, her death was a very long good bye.

---

[9] John Coolidge to Grace Coolidge, November 30, 1928, CCMF collection.
[10] Ibid.
[11] John Coolidge to Grace Coolidge, February 5, 1929, CCMF collection.
[12] Grace Coolidge to John Coolidge, May 15, 1929, CCMF collection.
[13] Bill Ryan, "Fall of '29: A Wedding to Remember in Plainville" *Hartford Courant*, June 8, 1986.
[14] Grace Coolidge to Pi Beta Phi Round Robins, October 4, 1929, Pi Beta Phi collection.
[15] Grace Coolidge to Maude Trumbull, January 29, 1930, CCMF collection.
[16] Grace Coolidge to Dr. and Mrs. Joel T. Boone, July 4, 1929, Library of Congress collection.

1929 was a memorable year for Calvin Coolidge. His son married and the president wrote his *Autobiography* which was published in serial form in *Cosmopolitan* magazine. He also was elected director of the New York Life Insurance Company. In the summer he attended a luncheon at the White House to celebrate the signing of the Kellogg-Briand Pact. 62 nations ultimately signed this treaty to outlaw war as a way of settling disputes. His intended legacy was to have served the people "who have honored me and the country which I love."[17]

Of course all of this was overshadowed by the stock market crash of 1929. Coolidge did not comment upon it publicly at the time. President Hoover did not call upon his predecessor for advice.[18] Coolidge's political isolation was difficult for him to understand. The 1932 convention did not even send greetings to him. Coolidge made two radio speeches on Hoover's behalf, one before a large gathering in Madison Square Garden. Yet he felt out of touch and did not even "fit...with these times."[19] The former president must have been quite dispirited. The Depression would not go away. The economic situation would sometimes improve only then to grow worse than before. One could not see the end of it. President Hoover, whom he had once referred to as the "wonder boy" because of his reputation for being able to handle all sorts of problems, was overwhelmed. Calvin, as a good and loyal Republican, had to find a way to be supportive and praise him for his fortitude and ask people to vote for him.

Calvin's writings in *American Magazine* were followed by those of Grace. She wrote her friends that while she was sewing and waiting for her husband one day, she started writing on her own. She expected her husband to dismiss her articles since she "submitted them to him for 'higher criticism,'" but he "approved of her efforts and became her agent taking them to New York for publication."[20] She realized that she was only being published because she was a wife of a president and she had no "inflated ideas about" her ability to write.[21]

Her husband was approached to write a syndicated column for McClure Newspaper Syndicate. This daily column would require heading to his office most days in downtown Northampton and with one hundred newspapers signed up, he would receive $203,045 for the year. Coolidge had much he wanted to say and he worked hard at producing these daily observations; their retirement was financially secure. In these articles he did deal with the subject of the economic

---

[17] *The Autobiography of Calvin Coolidge*, p. 247.
[18] Sobel, p. 408.
[19] Ibid, p. 410.
[20] Grace Coolidge to Pi Beta Phi Round Robin, July 4, 1929, Pi Beta Phi archives.
[21] Ibid.

depression. He inveighed, "My countrymen, it is time to stop criticizing and quarreling and begin sympathizing and helping."[22]

In recognition of her advocacy and community service, Grace received four honorary degrees from Boston University, Smith College, George Washington University, and, in 1930, the University of Vermont, her alma mater. The citation at the University of Vermont read, in part, "All ours when the school girl lived and worked among us; ours still though not unshared when the First Lady cast her kindly spell of act and speech and manner over the hearts of a nation; ours now when we honor in her guise the crown of achievement, the art of arts, the power of grace, the magic in a name."[23] One of the graduates on the stage that day recalled fondly, "There was no way one could ever forget her or not love her."[24]

Living in half of a two family house became unbearable. The Coolidges needed more room and a yard with an iron fence to keep in the dogs and keep away the curious. In May of 1930, Calvin and Grace moved to the Beeches, a house with 13 rooms and a detached garage. The house had four fireplaces and natural wood detailing around the doors and stairways.[25] The six acres of grounds had a wading pool, tennis court, and gazebo with perennial gardens and a rose garden. Grace wrote her friends that she was worried if she would grow to like it, since her roots had gone down so deep at Massasoit Street. "Somehow, I feel that it is only a temporary home, like the Adirondacks or South Dakota—or even the White House—but then, they are all temporary. And sometimes, I tell this only to you [Dr. Boone], I feel that when I get things a little bit settled here and everything going smoothly, maybe my work will be done."[26] On the first floor she had a living room with "glassed in and screened sun porch, a medium sized dining room, a too small library, a lavatory and coat closet, kitchen and pantries." On the second floor there were two master bedrooms and "a large screened sleeping porch."[27] Her husband could "smoke and read without fear of observation."[28] She could have "her own work room upstairs, where she typed her letters, sewed and knitted, read and attended to her pets."[29] She slept on an upper porch "and I awake in the morning with the sun streaming in upon me and the birds twittering and chattering in the branches of the trees. Lovely, lovely world."[30]

---

[22] Fuess, p. 449.
[23] Susan Webb, "Grace Goodhue Coolidge" *The Real Calvin Coolidge # 10*, p. 21.
[24] Ibid.
[25] Daisy Mathias and Robert Nelson, "The Beeches," *The Real Calvin Coolidge # 5*, p. 27.
[26] Grace Coolidge to Dr. Joel T. Boone, June 26, 1930, Library of Congress collection.
[27] Grace Coolidge to Round Robins, July 4, 1930, Pi Beta Phi archives.
[28] Ross, p. 270.
[29] Ibid.
[30] Grace Coolidge to Dr. Joel T. Boone, June 26, 1930, Library of Congress collection.

Grace was again to feel the romantic side of her husband. When they were first dating, he wrote many letters to Grace with compliments. Now, with the White House behind them, he took time to celebrate their anniversary. He arranged a private dinner in 1930, at the Wayside Inn, a favorite spot steeped in colonial history. Grace wrote in her round robin correspondence, this was "another adventure into dreamland."[31] Her husband wrote to her from the Vanderbilt Hotel where he was at a meeting without her, "I wish I was home."[32] He wrote "My dear Grace" and signed off 'with much love" and wrote on December 8, 1932 from the same hotel, "I have thought of you all the time since I left home."[33]

"As he grows older I think he will turn more and more to these peaceful hills (of Plymouth, Vermont). It is in the Coolidge blood and I think you will all agree that where he leads I follow..."[34] Calvin had definite plans to make Plymouth more hospitable and to extend their time there during the colder weather. A separate wing was added to the homestead. Electricity and a flush bathroom were added in 1932. One of their goals was to make the house more comfortable for guests as well. Grace was preparing for a visit from Governor and Mrs. Trumbull, the in-laws of her son, John. She wrote, "The lean-to, as Mr. Coolidge has called the new wing, in referring to it, is far from complete, as far as furnishings go, but there is everything essential, and I think we can make you comfortable. Mr. Coolidge does things when he gets around to it and I do not make him uncomfortable nor myself unhappy by urging him—as I told John, it is his wing and I am letting him flap it."[35] Grace also wrote to her friend Ivah Gale about the new wing. "Across the front is one long living room, paneled on the windowside with book shelves from floor to ceiling on the other three sides with a large brick fireplace opposite the door. Back of this are our bedrooms and a bath room and linen closet across the end in a screened porch, a third of it—the end leading from my bedroom door is partitioned off for my sleeping porch..."[36] Her husband got up early to supervise the workmen. Tourists still "throng the place" so the quiet they sought was often disrupted.[37] Grace had found peace and beauty back in Vermont. She wrote, "As the dusk deepens into night and the moon shines across the meadows and against the hills, there is a glory over it all which causeth the

---

[31] Grace Coolidge to Round Robins, November 8, 1930, CCMF Collection
[32] Calvin Coolidge to Grace Coolidge, November 11, 1929, Coolidge Family Papers, Vermont Historical Society.
[33] Ibid, December 12, 1932.
[34] Grace Coolidge to Round Robins, September 26, 1931, Pi Beta Phi archives.
[35] Grace Coolidge to Maude Trumbull, September 27, 1932, CCMF Collection.
[36] Grace Coolidge to Ivah Gale, September 29, 1932, Ivah Gale Collection Collection
[37] Grace Coolidge to Teresa Hills, July 28, 1931, Forbes Library.

spirit within to take flight and approach almost to the gate of heaven...White puffs of cloud floated about and I wished that Maxfield Parish would paint such a picture."[38] Grace was becoming very attached to Plymouth.

Grace had a struggle overseeing her husband's health. Frank W. Stearns had written that Calvin had "backwoods ideas on medicine, will only take medical advice when he sees fit to do so, and will rarely see fit to do so."[39] As president, Calvin did take walks for exercise after Dr. Boone urged him to do so. In retirement, Coolidge confided to an Amherst classmate, in 1933, "I am very comfortable because I am not doing anything of any account; but a real effort to accomplish anything goes hard with me. I am too old for my years. I suppose the carrying of responsibilities as I have done takes its toll. I'm afraid I'm burned out. But I am very comfortable."[40] The classmate, Charles Andrews, thought Coolidge "looked tired." Grace observed that he was "easily fatigued and walked slowly" and he used a spray for his asthma.[41] She also believed that "the death of our younger son was a severe shock and the zest of living never was the same to him afterward."[42] Frank Buxton, a friend, toured Plymouth with Calvin that fall but observed a changed man, "His face was drawn and pale. He moved slowly and wearily. He ate sparingly."[43] He took two naps a day and had "recurring attacks of what was diagnosed as asthma" and had digestive troubles.[44] "The man of 59 looked as his father looked at seventy," it was observed.[45]

Grace saw her husband's concern for his legacy, yet she also saw him take joy in his current projects. She worried that a new book called *The Rise of Saint Calvin, Merry Sidelights on the Career of Mr. Coolidge* had upset him. She told a friend "that her husband had something on his mind which was bothering him terribly and that she was trying to learn what it was."[46] Charles B. Hayes, Field Director of the American Foundation for the Blind, visited with Calvin during the same time period and declared that he seemed "jolly". The former president seemed to really enjoy his philanthropy for people with disabilities.

The Coolidge office routine never wavered. You could set your watch on it. But on January 5, 1933, after a short time at the office, Calvin and his chauffeur returned to the Beeches, then offered the car to Grace who turned it down

---

[38] Ibid.
[39] Heller, p. 82.
[40] Sobel, p. 412.
[41] Ibid., p. 413.
[42] William Allen White, *A Puritan in Babylon* (New York: The Macmillan Company, 1938), p. 434.
[43] Ibid., p. 431.
[44] White, p.432.
[45] Ibid., p. 435.
[46] Fuess, p. 463.

preferring to walk to town instead. Checking on the work of a boiler repairman, Calvin then walked upstairs to shave at about noon and a few minutes later, Grace came up the stairs and found her husband dead from a coronary thrombosis.[47] There was nothing she could do. At least with Calvin Jr. she had been there with him as he slipped away fighting his blood poisoning. This time she was shocked without enough clues to see her husband's decline. He constantly had his pulse taken and was good about talking to doctors, but did tend to himself a lot and did bottle up his thoughts about his declining health.

As the world learned of the death of her husband through her initial release of information and the publication in newspapers, Calvin's loyal friends were distraught. The housekeeper at the Plymouth Notch homestead, Aurora Pierce, "buried her face in her hands" and Frank Stearns was speechless and then drove to Northampton to wait for the funeral.[48] "A more understanding, sympathetic, considerate and kind man, I have [n]ever known," lamented Hillsy.[49] Hillsy stayed with her neighbor, Grace, watching over her as she cried for two nights.[50] Miss Randolph, Grace's secretary from the White House, came to sort and classify telegrams, letters, and cards. Grace, herself, wrote out notes which "demand a personal touch."[51]

On a national level, President Herbert Hoover, a lame-duck awaiting the swearing in of president-elect Franklin D. Roosevelt, sent a special message to Congress and ordered thirty days of public mourning. Congress adjourned.[52] Grace decided against an official funeral in Washington.[53] She wanted a funeral in Northampton with burial in Plymouth. She thought that her husband would not have wanted a formal state funeral since he had already retired and was living a relatively quiet life. He had wanted to "return to the people," as he had written in his autobiography.[54]

Grace and John quickly planned the service with the pastor of the Edwards Church in Northampton, Massachusetts. When Saturday came, crowds started gathering early since they could pass the coffin from 8:30 a.m. to 9:30 a.m. and thousands did. This was the largest crowd the city of Northampton ever experienced, according to eye witness accounts. The Coolidge pew was draped

---

[47] Ibid., p. 464.
[48] Ibid.
[49] "Calvin Coolidge: As Northampton Knew Him", newspaper article found at Edwards Church dated January 1, 1958.
[50] Grace Coolidge to Joel T. Boone, January 16, 1933, Library of Congress collection.
[51] Ibid.
[52] Fuess, p. 464.
[53] Ross, p. 288.
[54] *The Autobiography of Calvin Coolidge*, p. 242.

with roses and ribbon. The open casket showed a weary face.[55] When the dignitaries came to the church for the funeral service, state police had to clear a path for President Hoover, wife of the President elect, Mrs. Franklin D. Roosevelt, members of the Supreme Court, Congressional members, and governors of adjoining states. The crowd stayed back in respect for the Coolidges, the Stearns family and former Senator Butler who entered together. The pallbearers were Frank Stearns, William F. Whiting, William M. Butler, Charles A. Andrews, former Governor John H. Trumbull, Judge John C. Hammond, R.B. Hills, Clifford Lyman and Walter L. Stevens. Whiting was the Secretary of Commerce from 1928-1929, William M. Butler had been Chairman of the National Republic Committee and a Senator from Massachusetts, Charles A. Andrews had been an Amherst classmate of Calvin's, Governor Trumbull was the father-in-law of John Coolidge, Judge John C. Hammond had been the partner of Calvin and a District Attorney, R.B. Hills was the husband of one of Grace's best friends, Teresa Hills, Clifford Lyman was a shopkeeper at Bridgman's bookshop in town, and Walter L. Stevens was a lawyer and member of Wednesday Club where Calvin had given talks and discussed politics.

Grace insisted that President Hoover return to Washington and not make the overland journey to Vermont, since the roads were dangerous in bad weather. Twenty cars made the procession of 100 miles to Plymouth's town cemetery. "In every village they went through, there were small troops of Boy Scouts and veterans of the Great War, standing at attention in silence as the motors sped by."[56] "Six sturdy U.S. Marshals bore the heavy coffin to the grave. "The young preacher's prayer was short....No band wailed, and the village watchers heard no song or psalm."[57] The last words said by the minister were "Good night, dear heart; good night, good night."[58] "A sudden storm of hail pelted down." [59] Grace had tried to smile in the morning coming out of the church in Northampton. Now she cried.[60] She reached out to John for steadying as she walked down the steep hill away from the grave.[61] Calvin's stone was next to Calvin Jr.'s, placed there in 1924. Calvin Coolidge, himself, had selected his stone to be the same composition and design as his deceased son's.

Grace Coolidge's unpublished poem about this setting must have given her some comfort with her expression of her grief.

---

[55] Fuess, p. 465.
[56] Clarence Day, *In the Green Mountain Country* (New Haven: Yale University Press, 1934) p. 6.
[57] White, p. 443.
[58] Author interview with John Coolidge, summer of 1999 in Plymouth, Vermont.
[59] Day, p. 7.
[60] Day, p. 8.

Communion

A quiet place, amid enfolding hills,
Green grass beneath my feet
And overhead, blue sky
With in between long, distances
To dream about;
Within a green-roofed house,
Sweet memories blessing every room;
Across the road, a small white church
Whose open door invites to prayer;
And, just around the turn,
On yonder hill, God's plot
Where sleep His dead-and mine-
Beneath two guardian pines;
So dear a place on earth,
So near the home called heaven;
And yet, the unwise ask,
Where is thy God.[62]

---

[61] Ross, p. 291.
[62] Lawrence E. Wikander, "Address to the Annual Meeting of the Calvin Coolidge Memorial Foundation on August 1, 1993"*The Real Calvin Coolidge #10*, p. 28.

Chapter 8

"Precious Four" and Life on Her Own

> "At heart, I am a simple, home-loving woman. I love best of all to gather my little family under my own roof and stay there." [1]

Grace Coolidge returned to Northampton right after the burial of her husband in Plymouth, Vermont.[2] His death at age 60 left her a relatively young widow of 54. Many more memorial services were held across the country and newspaper editorials "gave Coolidge more generous appraisal than he had received in his lifetime."[3] He had presided over an era of prosperity which they all wished could come again. Grace was often praised as well in these commentaries. She was fondly remembered by the nation.

Grace was financially comfortable. Calvin's will, like the man, was most concise and to the point. "Not unmindful of my son John, I give all my estate, both real and personal, to my wife, Grace Coolidge, in fee simple."[4] A trust had been arranged for John when he married Florence Trumbull. Calvin left $700,000, a tidy sum saved by a man who rarely spent money.

Grace wrote Maude Trumbull at the end of January, the same month as that of her husband's death, "I am glad you like the photograph of Calvin. I think it is one of his best. Having a photograph taken was always a serious matter with him and most of his studio pictures are very serious—often stern. Life was always a serious matter with him. He never felt the need of "play"—wouldn't have known how to satisfy the need if he had recognized it. Early in our acquaintance I tried to teach him and sometimes he made an effort to respond but usually tried to show

---

[1] *Grace Coolidge: An Autobiography*, p. 110.
[2] Ross, p. 291.
[3] Ibid.
[4] Ross, p. 293.

me how important it was to face life in a serious manner. I am so thankful that it was given me to see him through."[5]

Grace portrayed herself in her letters as the one who helped her husband cope with his life as his safety valve. Yet her friend Frances Keyes thought Grace lost her "purpose and mainspring when her husband died" since she had "leaned on him" in a way.[6] She had made no plans for herself. She had always been available to take care of his needs. Calvin's career had been paramount and she and the boys had had to adjust. Some of the events were wonderful and joyful, and some were stressful. She had lived her life out in the public glare. Yet she kept correspondence going with fraternity sisters, with her Northampton friends and her UVM "sister", Ivah Gale, for life. Still, this warm and friendly woman "somehow managed to keep her personal relationships private to a remarkable degree."[7] She took so much joy in her son's family. Her faith sustained her, as she wrote in so many letters. More than that, as she often said, people were her books, meaning that her interest in people kept her going. In Northampton she knew people to speak with in stores and on the street. "She not only remembered their names, but also the names of their spouses and children."[8] She elicited the opinions of others on subjects of interest to her and rarely offered her own opinion. She was always a meticulous dresser still enjoying navy blue and a rich shade of red.[9]

She was free to pursue her own interests. In February, she left with Mrs. Florence Adams, her neighbor in Northampton, to live several months in Columbia, North Carolina and this was to become a pattern for future winters. Grace enjoyed the company of a very strong opinionated woman in Florie Adams. She was a New Deal Democrat, wealthy, and rather liberated. She had graduated from Smith College in 1905 and returned to earn an MA in history in 1930 there.[10] She had married, divorced, and raised a daughter, Janey. She was a neighbor who remembered the young Coolidge family and answering the door to see ten year old Calvin Jr. asking to borrow a book.

Grace enjoyed her time in the mountains hiking, sleeping outside, playing cards, and working on crossword puzzles. Life there was "carefree and the

---

[5] Grace Coolidge to Maude Trumbull, January 30, 1933, CCMF Collection.
[6] Ross, p. 293.
[7] Unpublished book review in the archives of Pi Beta Phi Fraternity, summer, 1962.
[8] Lydia Coolidge Sayles, "Grace Coolidge, My Grandmother," *The New England Journal of History*, Vol. 55, No. 1, Fall 98, p. 80.
[9] Larry Parnass and Phoebe Mitchell, "In Praise of Grace Coolidge"*Daily Hampshire Gazette*, July 30, 1999.
[10] "Obituary" *Daily Hampshire Gazette*, Northampton, MA, February 12, 1973, Smith College archives. She wrote a book about Fanny Fern, a 19th century American journalist.

problems confronting the world" seemed so far away and unimportant.[11] Grace immersed herself in this world of Smith graduates, "a most interesting group whom I enjoyed immensely and who accepted me as one of them."[12] Florie Adams lived with Florence Snow of the Smith College Alumnae Association. Florence was a graduate of the class of 1904 and was the first resident officer of the Association; she retired as its general secretary emeritus in 1948. She also was a prize-winning amateur photographer.[13]

Teresa Hills was not part of this circle. Hillsy complained to Joel Boone, "For over twenty years—I have seen her every day [when Grace was in Northampton] and it is a bit hard getting adjusted to this new way."[14]

Grace found herself in this very new world without staff or a husband. She wrote Dr. Boone, "I shall try to get along without anybody (regarding staff). With the Plymouth properties on my hands and this place here, my time is fully occupied and my problems many and varied. However, it is well for me to be busy and to keep the old mind active. I am getting some experience in affairs which I have never known anything about."[15] She even urged the Boones to move to Massasoit Street to be near her and to have access to good schools for Suzanne. They did not do it, but this indicated how much Grace wanted to draw old friends and staff very close.

Joy came to Grace once again when she became a grandmother. Cynthia was born to John and Florence Coolidge on October 1, 1933. In her letters, Grace fairly exhaled her joy at another wonderful human event. She wrote to Maude Trumbull, "I can realize how eager you were to see Cynthia. I think she is a wonderful baby and I am sure it is not entirely due to the fact that I share grandmothership with you. Florence is a beautiful mother....How her Grandfather Coolidge would have loved her! He liked girls and wanted one of his own."[16] Grace enjoyed her new role. She now had a little girl to dress up and spoil! Since John's family was in Connecticut, she could visit them fairly easily. She still did not drive herself, but had a chauffeur or friends drive her. John Bukosky, the Polish chauffeur, had driven the Coolidges ever since they left the White House.[17] "Johnny-Jump-Up" was his nickname and he helped with the gardens as well.

Headlines were once again focusing on a Coolidge romance. This time they got wind of Everett Sanders' interest in Grace Coolidge; he was Calvin

---

[11] Grace Coolidge to Dr. Joel T. Boone, May 31, 1934, Library of Congress collection.
[12] Grace Coolidge to John Coolidge, April 22, 1934, CCMF collection
[13] Information provided by the Smith College archives, Smith College News Office.
[14] Teresa Hills to Dr. Joel T. Boone, May 24, 1934, Library of Congress collection.
[15] Grace Coolidge to Dr. Joel T. Boone, September 7, 1933, Library of Congress collection.
[16] Grace Coolidge to Maude Trumbull, September 21, 1934, CCMF Collection.

Coolidge's former presidential secretary and Chairman of the National Committee. Biographer Ishbel Ross reported that Grace "weighed the question."[18] Rumors surfaced while Grace was at the mountain retreat in North Carolina and she wrote her son about them. She faced it all with good humor even cutting out a newspaper headline, "Where's Grandma Tonight" to write her son, "Here she is, safe and sound and single, and in so far as she is aware, in her right mind. Somebody went crazy but it was not she."[19] One reporter tracked her down in the mountains assuming she was on her honeymoon!

Grace wrote many letters and increased her volume after she left the White House. It must have been quite a day when she was granted a franking privilege. She would do quite nicely with it. She wrote her son, "I received notice from the Postmaster-General one day last week that the President had signed the bill granting me the franking privilege and that I was henceforth entitled to send matter through the mails free. Graft—eh? I wonder if I come under XY2 or KLM or what—must be there are some letters which apply or that I come under one code or another."[20] She was also poking fun at the proliferation of the Roosevelt administration's programs.

Grace Coolidge did not return to the capital in a public way as other first ladies had done. She preferred to travel "under the radar screen." She did not have a need to meet the high and mighty. In December of 1934, Grace and Florie Adams traveled through Washington to reach their winter retreat. They toured the capital as tourists might and only one traffic officer recognized her![21] However, on another trip to Stockbridge, Massachusetts, she was escorted to the box at a symphonic festival to meet "Madam Roosevelt", as she called her in correspondence, so she did occasionally cross paths with the leaders of our nation.[22]

In 1934 and 1935, Grace Coolidge asked a group of men and women who had known her husband to write reminiscences about him for *Good Housekeeping* magazine. This was important for her since she was really shaping the legacy of her husband by asking for these eye-witness written accounts by fifty people. She also commented on each article herself. She even chose Alfred E. Smith, a Democrat and opponent of Herbert Hoover in 1928, as her first eye witness.[23] She

---

[17] Ross, p. 336.
[18] Ross, p. 297.
[19] Grace Coolidge to John Coolidge, April 23, 1934, CCMF Collection.
[20] Grace Coolidge to John Coolidge, June 25, 1934, CCMF Collection.
[21] Grace Coolidge to John Coolidge, November 30, 1934, CCMF collection.
[22] Grace Coolidge to John Coolidge, August 15, 1935, CCMF collection.
[23] Grace Coolidge, "The Real Calvin Coolidge", *Good Housekeeping* magazine, February 1935, p. 20.

willingly shared materials with the public, even her husband's last letter to her from New York City. The public was getting a different picture of Calvin Coolidge; she was warming up his image considerably. As Bernard Baruch wrote, Coolidge was "very shy, but always considerate of his associates."[24] He did not discuss himself and "had all the human qualities" that Dwight Morrow had, his dear friend from his Amherst class.[25] Baruch was also a Democrat and Calvin appreciated him since "we needed a two-party system in order that one could criticize and check the other."[26] Grace revealed some intimate details of her life such as the fact that her husband rarely gave her gifts or celebrated anniversaries. She wrote, "Mr. Coolidge had deeper sentimental feeling than most people whom I have known, but he did not reveal it in outward manifestations."[27]

Grace had been the adventurous one in the couple. She finally took a plane flight with Governor Trumbull, "an enthusiastic aviator who went up in his plane every Sunday."[28] She was game for new things. Her son commented that she did look for new and different things in life.

Grace's had always wanted to travel in Europe, but never could interest her husband. In 1936, she and Florie Adams plunged in and decided to visit the Adams' daughter, Janey, studying in London, and travel again unrecognized to soak up the sounds, smells, views, and history of Europe and the British Isles. Florie was the trusty driver of an "Auburn convertible phaeton" they named Oliver. "They traveled like two young college girls, picnicking at times, exploring out of the way places, taking things as they came, and always Mrs. Coolidge maintained the utmost good humor."[29] Grace wrote,

> "I have fully decided that circumstances which worked together to make it possible for me to take a trip to Europe have favored me for I am sure that it is all meaning a great deal more to me now than if I had come when younger and life was all before me. Further, I am fortunate in having Florie for a companion, guide and friend—as well as chauffeur. She has covered a great deal of it before and hesitates at nothing."[30]

---

[24] Ibid., p. 182.
[25] Ibid.
[26] Ibid., p. 183.
[27] Ibid., p. 191.
[28] Ross, p. 304.
[29] Ross., p. 306.
[30] Grace Coolidge to John Coolidge, March 9, 1936, CCMF Collection.

Grace was also game for anything. She wrote that she pulled a wire they ran over out of a tire with pliers.[31] She was resourceful! However, she was aware of the military tensions in the air, but the "League of Nations seems to be muddling along as usual."[32] "We keep a reserve of French francs in our jeans," she wrote just in case they had to make a fast exit.[33] "What a mess Europe is in, and what is going to happen?"[34] They "motored nearly 12,000 miles, the last three weeks in Holland, Denmark and Sweden."[35] Her diplomatic passport seemed to smooth the way at many borders.

While Grace was out of the country, she had authorized an auction of "home furnishings" from 21 Massasoit Street and the Beeches as a benefit to the Hampshire County Chapter of the American Red Cross.[36] She felt that New England families often offer "for sale what is not wanted by the heirs" and she was paring down to prepare to sell the Beeches.[37] She had already moved out to live with Florie Adams and Florence Snow at 112 Washington Street. The auctioneer arranged items at the Smith school arena with 400 attending and an admission price of one dollar. Judge Henry P. Field, a mentor of Calvin Coolidge, was "sorry it was held" since it sent a message that "valuable furniture of Calvin Coolidge" was being sold.[38] In reality, the historic items had already been given to Forbes Library, a public library in Northampton Calvin had chosen to receive important artifacts. Grace did not realize that the presidency had become such a public domain and souvenir hunters would want to claim anything to do with fame and fortune. The auction included 400 items including a dining room set, rockers, wardrobes, bookshelves, Victrola records, and the desk used by Calvin Coolidge.[39] Grace wrote her son from Europe, "I have seen some of the publicity which I have not liked very much…I am sure that I did not let him have anything which you could possibly want. There are no antiques I can assure you."[40]

Although Grace did not expect or ask for any pension, in 1937, Senator Carter Glass introduced a bill giving her a pension of $5,000 a year.[41] Elizabeth Jaffrey, the White House housekeeper, had commented that middle class presidents had to

---

[31] Grace Coolidge to John Coolidge, April 26, 1936, CCMF Collection.
[32] Grace Coolidge to John Coolidge, Mary 3, 1935, CCMF collection.
[33] Ibid.
[34] Grace Coolidge to Joel T. Boone, September 18, 1936, Library of Congress Collection.
[35] Ibid.
[36] Memorabilia in archives, The Calvin Coolidge Memorial Foundation.
[37] Ibid.
[38] Ibid.
[39] Ernestine Perry, *Springfield Union* newspaper, May, 1936, The Calvin Coolidge Memorial Foundation archives.
[40] Grace Coolidge to John Coolidge, April, 1936, CCMF collection.
[41] Ross, p. 307.

"Precious Four" and Life on Her Own

find a way to make money after the White House. They needed to write as Calvin Coolidge had done or work for companies to provide for their families. Pensions were often voted in for widowed first ladies who had lost their husbands.

In 1938 Grace sold the Beeches to Mary Bailey.[42] Grace Coolidge still wanted her own home and built one she called "Road Forks" across from that of Florie Adams on Ward Avenue with "beautiful trees around it."[43] The home was unusual since the living quarters were on the second floor. The first floor was for parking.[44] She had a store room with a vault there as well. Her third floor included a guest room, maid's room and sleeping porch. She was avoiding prying eyes again. In these times, no Secret Service protection was provided.

Pleased that her son was also building a house, Grace helped him with it financially. He also had a new addition to his family. Lydia was born on August 14, 1939. She was a "fine, healthy, happy baby who gave promise of having red hair."[45] The red hair would show evidence of the president's sandy color in the genes. So the sixty year old grandmother would have two girls to play with now! She also needed to help her own son since he had a sudden operation and was told to spend more time out-of-doors and take "a six month leave of absence."[46] Grace kept her upbeat attitude and wrote, "he'll have to step some to keep up with the old gal."[47] John had worked for the New York, New Haven and Hartford Railroad for twelve years and then became president of Connecticut Manifold Forms in West Hartford, Connecticut in 1941. His father-in-law was governor of Connecticut from 1925 to 1931. John and Florence were not actively interested in politics as their parents had been. They liked living in small towns where they could be outdoors to play tennis and ride horses.

Grace loved her community work, especially for the Clarke School for the Deaf in Northampton. In 1929, she presented a two million dollar fund, raised by Coolidge admirers as a parting tribute to the Coolidges at the end of the administration, to the Clarke School. It was used to create the Clarence W. Barron Research Department which would study experimental phonetics, the heredity of deafness, and the psychological difficulties of the deaf child.[48] She often visited the school and checked on the scientific advances. In 1931, she received a medal for "distinguished social services" from the National Institute for Social

---

[42] Daisy Mathias and Robert Nelson, "The Beeches" *The Real Calvin Coolidge #5*, p. 29.
[43] Grace Coolidge to Joel T. Boone, January 4, 1938, Library of Congress Collection.
[44] Ross, p. 308.
[45] Grace Coolidge to Joel T. Boone, January 4, 1940, Library of Congress Collection.
[46] Grace Coolidge to Joel T. Boone, January 15, 1941, The Library of Congress Collection.
[47] Ibid.
[48] Charlene McPhail Anderson,"Grace Coolidge and the Clarke School for the Deaf," *The Real Calvin Coolidge #10*, p. 10.

Sciences.[49] In 1935, she was head of the board of trustees at the Clarke School and represented the school for presentations such as dedicating a building in honor of her former principal, Caroline Yale. She began another fund raising drive in 1955 for three million dollars to improve the school. She helped form a committee with Helen Keller, Christian A. Herter, Leverett Saltonstall, Spencer Tracy, Herbert Hoover, Jr., and Claude M. Fuess serving with her.[50] She enjoyed her association with John F. Kennedy, her fellow trustee and another advocate for the deaf. She helped grow the school to over 17 buildings on a twenty acre campus. She watched over the most advanced efforts to use electronics to help deaf children. She could often be seen visiting classes, eating in the dining room, having tea in the Coolidge building after the Christmas sale or attending board meetings at Hubbard Hall.[51] All the children knew her by name.

Inheriting the Plymouth properties after the death of her husband, Grace was determined to maintain Calvin's boyhood home during the Depression and World War II. She relied heavily on Aurora Pierce, the housekeeper who cared for Calvin's father for forty years and lived on in the homestead after his death. The Plymouth housekeeper was "ferociously neat and tidy" even scrubbing the floor so hard in the kitchen that it lost its paint![52] Aurora, in her eighties, was keeping the house well cared for as she expected summer visits from Grace Coolidge and her son's family of four. Aurora gardened and canned or jarred vegetables for winter meals. Grace often wrote the Charles Hoskison family, tenants on the Coolidge farm, to remind them to watch over Aurora, their neighbor. "She said that she had to saw and chop wood in order to have any to burn," Grace wrote in 1943, urging the Hoskisons to help her.[53] Grace could not get to Plymouth when gas rationing was in effect.[54] Yet she paid the Hoskisons to make sure Aurora got meat and wood for the winter. As Grace wrote, "It must be a lonesome business, living there by herself through a Vermont winter."[55] In 1942, Grace sold trees around the farm writing that "it was my patriotic duty to sell these trees for the government needs paper."[56] She had two houses in Plymouth, the homestead and the farm, a quarter of a mile away from each other. She felt that Plymouth was

---

[49] Ibid.
[50] Ross, p. 312.
[51] Interview with Rodney Kunath, student at Clarke School for the Deaf, 1946-1958.
[52] Will and Jane Curtis, Frank Lieberman, *Return to These Hills, The Vermont Years of Calvin Coolidge* (Woodstock, Vermont: Curtis-Lieberman Books, 1985) p. 82.
[53] Grace Coolidge to Charles Hoskison, October 15, 1943, CCMF collection.
[54] Ibid.
[55] Grace Coolidge to Eliza Hoskison, December 13, 1940, CCMF collection.
[56] Grace Coolidge to Charles Hoskison, March 24, 1942, CCMF collection.

becoming a "deserted village with only four houses occupied" in 1947.[57] Aurora Pierce rarely threw anything out, so items from the 1920's were preserved for the ages including clothes and utensils that Calvin Coolidge and his family had used.

"Of course it will be quiet, with no other young people around, but the air is good, the food fair-to-middling! Sleeping excellent and a welcome as deep and wide as the universe," Grace wrote to her son and daughter–in-law in 1932.[58] She really did have a fond spot in her heart for Plymouth Notch, her husband's village, and tried to visit it every summer as did her son. "I shall go to Plymouth, at least for a couple of days, on the 2nd in order to be there on the 3rd when the Republican State Committee is planning a "home-coming-Memorial Exercises" I believe they call it. Senator Austin and Congressman James M. Beck are to speak and there will be a national radio hookup from 1:30 to 2:30. They expect Col. Lindbergh to fly over during the ceremony as he has expressed a wish to do so. This last is strictly confidential. They would like to have the sitting room open to visitors and I think I had better be there," she wrote her son on July 9, 1934.[59] Already Plymouth was becoming a central place to remember the legacy of her late husband. She brought her friends such as Hillsy up to Plymouth to picnic. Once there, she would look over repairs in the homes and even make suggestions to improve signs at the cemetery where one could view the gravestones of her family.

Grace saw the constant visitation to Plymouth and felt that she should help consider some type of memorial to her husband. "I am convinced that there is something here for which people are hungrily searching and I trust that some arrangement may be made whereby they may find inspiration and take away a measure of the strength and courage which our men and women of the past who have lived here have found to be sufficient to their needs. To this end I am prepared to co-operate in every way possible. No-one has asked me and it has not been suggested to me that I should deed this place to the State of Vermont. I am not sure that I could give it over entirely but some arrangement could easily be made whereby people might be admitted to that part of the house in which the scene of August 3rd, 1923 took place."[60] She concluded in this letter that she must confer with John since he is "deeply attached to this home."[61]

When war came, Grace supported the allies wholeheartedly. "In 1939 she raised funds to bring child refugees from Germany to the United States" and also

---

[57] Grace Coolidge to Eliza Hoskison, January 2, 1947, CCMF collection.
[58] Grace Coolidge to John Coolidge, August 1, 1932, CCMF collection.
[59] Grace Coolidge to John Coolidge, July 9, 1934, CCMF collection.
[60] Grace Coolidge to Mr. Buxton, August 22, 1934, CCMF collection.
[61] Ibid.

raised funds for the "Dutch victims of the Nazi invaders."[62] After Pearl Harbor in 1941, Grace "devoted herself energetically to war work, helping the Red Cross, the civil defense authorities and wartime drives of all kinds."[63] She wrote her fraternity sisters, "At last we take our place in this world conflict. How incredible it all seems!...it will be a long hard conflict which will call for the utmost effort upon the part of every one of us but we cannot doubt that the forces which have truth and right and justice on their side will win. May God give us wisdom and leaders who will know how to establish the new peace upon foundations which will uphold it for long, long years to come."[64] She helped maintain a 24 hour watch at the Warning Center by working each Monday and participated in a trial black out. She prepared Red Cross dressings, knitted and made "all sorts of garments" for the troops.[65] She was on the Northampton committee where they gave books, a box lunch, and cigarettes to the draftees as they left for camp—about twenty to fifty a month.[66]

Grace became almost the symbol of the Waves in Northampton from 1942 to 1945.[67] Smith College was the first Naval Training School for women officers. From 1942 to 1945, three dorms, one hall, part of the gym, and a wing of the Alumnae House were used by the Navy. Dining was at the Hotel Northampton. Grace loaned her home, Road Forks, to Captain Herbert W. and Mrs. Underwood while he was in command. They gave many parties at the house. Grace kept her car at her house and Johnny, her chauffeur, stayed to help out. Nine thousand women were trained in Northampton and some were from the Pi Beta Phi fraternity as well.[68] The former first lady traveled with the Underwoods to review the Waves at Hunter College in New York City.

She moved back to Mrs. Adams house so she could loan the house to the Waves. In 1944, Florie Adams moved to New York to be near her daughter and new grandchild in Princeton, New Jersey; Florence Snow moved back to the Smith dorms; and Grace rented a small house until the war was over. As Grace wrote, "I have started over so many lives that I feel I should have some helpful suggestions to make."[69] In 1945, Florie Adams returned to Northampton and joined Grace as she re-opened her Road Forks home after the Underwoods had left. Florie would open up her own house when she could manage the expense and

---

[62] Ross, p. 314.
[63] Ross, p. 315.
[64] Grace Coolidge to Pi Beta Phi sisters, December 12, 1941, CCMF collection.
[65] Grace Coolidge to Charles Hoskison, August 11, 1942, CCMF collection.
[66] Grace Coolidge to Pi Beta Phi sisters, September 11, 1942, CCMF collection.
[67] Ross, p. 315.
[68] The Tercentenary Committee, *The Northampton Book*, p. 324.
[69] Grace Coolidge to Pi Beta Phi sisters, August 1, 1944, CCMF collection.

furnace work. The war was still impacting the women with a lack of meat and very little butter available.[70] Grace was getting a bit more outspoken. She admitted to arguing with a woman who advocated America First, the isolationist committee, but since it was so late in the war, this was hardly controversial.

In 1946, Grace invited Ivah Gale to come and live with her.

> "Dearest Ivah,
>
> For once in your life you are to do exactly as you please and have a little fun, I hope. You have always lived for others and I want you to do a little living for yourself now. Call this place "home" and go and come as you please. You may starve because, as you know, I am no cook and my own meals are sketchy but we can always get our main meal down the street and I find that rather a good idea because it is so difficult to get food in the markets. We are told that conditions in that line will grow worse before they get better."[71]

Ivah had lived with Grace on Maple Street for two years during their University of Vermont years and was a Pi Phi as well. Grace always treated her as a sister and wrote her quite often over the years. Ivah was single and had lived with a brother and his invalid wife. It was when that did not work out that Grace offered her a home. Ivah was partially deaf and shy but also "the most unselfish person" Grace knew, so she was pleased to invite her to be part of her extended family in Northampton.[72] Grace encouraged her to take lip reading at the Clarke School for the Deaf in case she totally lost her hearing. Of course Grace was the more active one. Her social life included trips, for example, to Falmouth, Basin Harbor, and Plymouth Notch in the summer of 1951. She liked to swim and fish.

Florie Adams had a change in her living circumstances as well. Her daughter divorced her husband and moved back to Northampton with Anne, age four, and David, age two. Grace felt she was an extra grandmother to these children. So now both Florie and Grace had enlarged their circle.

Always the good fund raiser, Grace took on two projects after the war. She raised funds for the Smith College 75th Anniversary fund as an honorary degree recipient and was chairman of the organ fund for Edwards Church. She claimed to "hate" fund raising but seemed willing to solicit funds when needed for the projects she believed in.[73]

---

[70] Grace Coolidge to Pi Beta Phi sisters, June 22, 1945, CCMF collection.
[71] Grace Coolidge to Ivah Gale, September 17, 1946, Ivah Gale collection.
[72] Grace Coolidge to Pi Beta Phi sisters, October 22, 1946, CCMF collection.
[73] Ibid, January 31, 1947.

One of Grace's favorite pastimes was still baseball! She loved to go to the games, or listen to them on the radio while doing her needlepoint projects. The American League sent her handbags with season passes each year, and she was happy to plan an outing to see the Red Sox. In 1950, she, at age 71, and Florie went to Camden, New Jersey to see a playoff game.[74] Grace arranged with Red Sox manager Joe Cronin for a special day for "deaf children" from Clarke School to attend a game. Grace listened so intently to the baseball games play by play she "practically folded up when they are over."[75] She even attended a baseball father and son banquet at Edwards Church since Joe Coleman, the Philadephia A's right-hander, was the guest speaker! She was the one who asked the most questions and fielded the correct answer when Coleman was stumped by a question of whether there was a triple play in a World Series (Bill Wambsganss, Cleveland infielder in 1920).[76] Several times a year, Florie Adams and Dr. Collins would join Grace for an outing to Boston for a game. She was even miffed that President Eisenhower, in 1953, could not take the time to throw out the first ball to start the season in Washington![77]

Grace always had her "precious four" in mind; John and his wife Florence and their two children, Cynthia and Lydia. John always remembered birthdays; he never forgot to send flowers to his mother on April 13, the date of his late brother's birthday. The grandmother was delighted when they built a new house in Farmington, Connecticut after the war. She joined them and the Trumbull grandparents for holidays, especially Christmas. She loved to shop with the girls and thoroughly spoiled them. She traveled with the family to Plymouth Notch each summer and since Aurora Pierce still ruled the roost, Grace "refereed" disagreements between Aurora and Florence.[78]

Grace had a physical fitness routine. She liked to hike in North Carolina or in Vermont. With Grace's walking schedule of six to eight miles a day, granddaughter Lydia had trouble keeping up with her. Grace instilled her love of auctions in the girls as well. In Northampton the girls saw evidence of Grace's hobbies such as tending to African violets and her collection of enamel and glass hands, "the most expressive part of the body."[79] Grace once wrote to her family, "I love best of all to gather my little family under my own roof and to stay here.

---

[74] Grace Coolidge to Ivah Gale, September 30, 1950, Ivah Gale collection.
[75] Ibid.
[76] David Pietrusza, "Grace Coolidge—The First Lady of Baseball," *The Real Calvin Coolidge #10*, p. 33.
[77] Ibid., p. 26.
[78] Lydia Coolidge Sayles, "Grace Coolidge, My Grandmother," *The New England Journal of History*, Vol. 55, No. 1, 1998, p. 79.
[79] Ibid., p. 80.

We are just a plain New England family and we like, above all else, to live and do the things that simple New England families do."[80] Granddaughter Cynthia at 18 was a "self contained unit, not very forthcoming, while Lydia is a complete contrast, full of high spirits and ready for anything" at age 12.[81]

In the 1950s, in her seventies, Grace continued to follow politics and culture. She was an avid reader who offered reviews of books to her sorority sisters on a regular basis. She quietly slipped into New York for the theatre or went to Boston where she was unrecognized.

Grace Coolidge, 1952 (CCMF archives)

In 1952, at the age of 73, her health began to fail. Grace had a time in the hospital with a heart attack and had an elevator installed in Road Forks. Ivah helped her and "country girls" came to the house to cook and do general housework. Finally the active first lady succumbed to watching television in 1954. In 1955, she was "chucked into an oxygen tent for a couple of days" on a health emergency.[82] She seldom went to Plymouth or for her daily walk. She could not even attend the 25th anniversary party of her son and daughter-in-law for fear of

---

[80] Ibid., p. 81.
[81] Grace Coolidge to Ellen Riley, August 15, 1951, Riley Papers.
[82] Grace Coolidge to Pi Beta Phi sisters, May 10, 1955, CCMF collection.

excitement! "Her knitting and her baseball, her books, her flowers, her radio, and her crossword puzzles kept her busy every minute..."[83] If she did go out, her car was fitted with special handles and a foot rest so she could get in and out of the car.

With the election of Dwight David Eisenhower, a Republican was back in the White House! First Lady Mamie Eisenhower's personal invitation to Grace to the festivities in 1953 delighted her, but she turned it down. She kept up her interest in the house itself writing Ellen Riley that "I cannot quite see the state dining room in green. I am glad the Eisenhowers are using the private dining room. I have always thought that was one of the most attractive rooms in the house and used to wish that we used it more."[84] "I read of the restoration of the fine old building and am happy to know that it will be preserved for future generations."[85]

Aurora Pierce died in the summer of 1956. A neighbor "found her lying on the floor."[86] They rushed her to the hospital but she did not recover. This was really the end of an era. Aurora had preserved the homestead with the help of Grace and John for these many years. John and his friends were considering forming a memorial foundation to help preserve the legacy of his father. His grandfather had often said that a memorial to his son, the 30th U.S. President, should be the village of Plymouth Notch. This was starting to take place. Those who revered the memory of Calvin Coolidge gathered on the homestead inaugural weekend, the first weekend of August, each year. So Grace and John gave the homestead to the state of Vermont with the stipulation that the state buy the birthplace of Calvin Coolidge across the street. The addition that President Coolidge had added to the homestead was moved to the farm where the first Coolidge began a settlement after the Revolutionary War. John was to build a cellar for it so he and his family could have a summer home in Plymouth.

The Coolidge grandchildren were growing up. Granddaughter Cynthia was studying at Bradford Junior College for two years after which she hoped to go to Mt. Holyoke College as her mother had done. "She is not a student of the first water, takes after her grandmother, I guess."[87] Cynthia went on to being a secretary at Trinity College. Lydia was to enter Bradford in the fall of 1957.

Grace's last public appearance was for the dedication of the Calvin Coolidge Memorial Room located in the Forbes Library in Northampton. At the ceremony, which took place at Smith College on September 16, 1956, Coolidge biographer

---

[83] Ross, p. 336-337.
[84] Grace Coolidge to Ellen Riley, February 9, 1953, Riley Papers.
[85] Grace Coolidge to Ellen Riley, August 15, 1951, Riley Papers.
[86] Grace Coolidge to Pi Beta Phi sisters, July 11, 1956, CCMF collection.
[87] Ibid, January 12, 1951.

Claude M. Fuess spoke, as did Massachusetts Governor Christian A. Herter. Forbes Library had been chosen by Calvin Coolidge as a repository for many of his papers and a special room had been formed with memorabilia on display. Most of his official Presidential papers had earlier been given to the Library of Congress.

In March of 1957, Grace's nurse wrote Joel Boone that she was very worried about her. She seemed to have lost "interest in anything at all." She only wanted to see her son, chauffeur Johnny, and Florie Adams.[88] In May, Grace's spirits picked up but she did not feel that she looked very well and did not want to see people. At 78 years old she went out to have her hair done and then retreated back into the house with three nurses to assist her.

Grace Coolidge died on July 8, 1957 of congestive heart and kidney failure. John and his family had stopped to see her on their way back from Plymouth Notch on July 7th. He drove his family home to Connecticut but turned right around to find she had just died on his return. She died just two hours from the 33rd anniversary of the death of her son Calvin Jr..

Funeral services were held at the Edwards Congregational Church. Contributions were to be made to the heart fund and the Clarke School for the Deaf. President Eisenhower named Senator Leverett Saltonstall of Massachusetts as his representative to the funeral and issued a public statement about her loss. The brief service of twenty minutes was attended by family and friends including Joel Boone of Washington, D.C. Bearers were business associate Harold L. Ames, George T. Pratt of the Clarke School, Lawrence E. Wikander, curator of the Coolidge Room at Forbes Library, business associate Franklin King Jr. of Williamsburg and John's boyhood friends: John H. Hills and Dr. Stephen Brown of Amherst. Reverend Richard Linde conducted the simple service with "some scriptural readings from Psalm 90, Proverbs 31, Corinthians 13, Grace's favorite hymns and her poem she wrote about the death of her son Calvin, "Open Door." The final simple rite of committing her ashes to the cemetery at Plymouth was done with only family and a few friends hovering in attendance. For sure, Florie Adams, Joel Boone, and Hillsy were close by. Grace's headstone was next to her husband's.

Remembrances of Grace Coolidge filled the Northampton papers. The mayor said they lost their "most prominent citizen."[89] Grace had been on the list of "America's 12 greatest living women."[90] The State Senate passed a resolution

---

[88] Edith N. Hill to Dr. Joel T. Boone, March 6, 1957, Library of Congress collection.
[89] "Mrs. Grace (Goodhue) Coolidge, Widow of 30th U.S. President Dies at Home in 79th Year" *The Hampshire Gazette*, July 8, 1957.
[90] *The Hampshire Gazette*, July 12, 1957.

recalling her as "a woman of personality, charm and dignity, a devoted mother and an inspirational wife and First Lady of the Land, of whom all people of our country were properly proud."[91] *The New York Times* ran this editorial: "Mrs. Calvin Coolidge must surely rank high in charm and dignity among the long line of White House hostesses who have graced that historic institution. Mrs. Coolidge's death yesterday cannot help but recall a glittering era in American history, the "Golden Twenties;" but her qualities of mind and heart represented something far deeper and more lasting in American life." *The Boston Globe* ran another editorial: "She was something new among Presidents' wives, an American working woman of the 20th century, the first mistress of the White House who could be distinctly identified as such."

All of this complimentary coverage was appreciated by friends and family. Yet Grace had stayed out for the spotlight for so long, refusing interviews or photographs. In the memorial service, Grace was recalled as a teacher of deaf children. One of her most important lessons was to get them to say "love" and to know what it meant. Grace Coolidge would have appreciated some of the headlines. She was heralded with "First Lady of Baseball" in many.

One of her poems found in her papers expresses her love for the American people, her family, and her God. What a fitting tribute to her life!

Watch-fires

Love was not given the human heart
For careless dealing
Its spark was lit that man
Might know Divine revealing.
Heaped up with sacrificial brands
The flame, in mounting
Enkindles other hearts with love
Beyond the counting.
Reflected back into each life
These vast fires, glowing
Do then become the perfect love
Of Christ's bestowing.[92]

---

[91] Ibid., July 9, 1957.
[92] Susan Webb, "Grace Goodhue Coolidge," *The Real Calvin Coolidge #10*, p. 21.

BIBLIOGRAPHY

PRIMARY COLLECTIONS

Claude M. Fuess Collection, Archives and Special Collections, Amherst College Library, Amherst, Massachusetts.
Frank Waterman Stearns Collection, Archives and Special Collections, Amherst College, Amherst, Massachusetts.
Archives, Edwards Church, Northampton, Massachusetts.
Calvin Coolidge Collection, Historic Northampton, Northampton, Massachusetts
Calvin Coolidge Collection, Forbes Library, Northampton, Massachusetts.
Grace Coolidge Papers, The Calvin Coolidge Memorial Foundation, Plymouth, Vermont.
Ivah Gale Collection, The Calvin Coolidge Memorial Foundation, Plymouth, Vermont.
Joel T. Boone Papers, Manuscript Division, Library of Congress, Washington, D.C.
Mercersburg Academy Archives, Mercersburg, Pennsylvania.
Pi Beta Phi Fraternity Archives, Town and Country, Missouri.
Riley Papers, Vermont Division for Historic Preservation Collection, Plymouth, Vermont.
Coolidge Family Papers, 1802-1932, Doc 215, Vermont Historical Society, Barre, Vermont.
"White House Days" (unpublished) extracts from the *Washington Post*, August 3,1923-March 5, 1929 compiled by Jozy Dell Hall, Coolidge Family Collection.

Published Works

Books

Anonymous. *The Mirrors of Washington*. New York: G.P. Putnam's Sons, 1921.

Anthony, Carl Sferrazza. *First Ladies, The Saga of the Presidents' Wives and Their Power, 1789-1961*. New York: William Morrow, 1990.

_____. *Florence Harding, the First Lady, the Jazz Age, and the Death of America's Most Scandalous President*. New York: William Morrow and Company, 1998.

Bryant, Blanche Brown. *Calvin Coolidge as I Knew Him*. DeLeon Springs, Florida: The E.O. Painter Printing Company, 1971.

Brown, Lance. *On the Road with Will Rogers*. Brunswick, Maine: Biddle Publishing Co., 1997.

Coit, Margaret L. *Mr. Baruch*. Cambridge, Massachusetts: The Riverside Press, 1957.

Coolidge, Calvin. *The Autobiography of Calvin Coolidge*. New York: Cosmopolitan Book Corporation, 1929.

_____. *Have Faith in Massachusetts*. Boston: Houghton Mifflin Company, 1919.

Coolidge, Grace. *Grace Coolidge: An Autobiography*. Worland, Wyoming: High Plains Press, 1992.

Curtis, Will and Jane, Lieberman, Frank. *Return to These Hills, The Vermont Years of Calvin Coolidge*. Woodstock, Vermont: Curtis-Lieberman Books, 1985.

Day, Clarence. *In the Green Mountain Country*. New Haven: Yale University Press, 1934.

Fischer, Margaret Jane. *Calvin Coolidge, Jr*. Rutland, Vermont: Academy Books, 1981.

Fuess, Claude M. *Amherst, the Story of a New England College*. Boston: Little Brown, and Co, 1935.

_____. *The Man from Vermont, Calvin Coolidge*. Boston: Little Brown and Company, 1940.

Gann, Dolly. *Dolly Gann's Book*. Garden City, New York: Doubleday, Doran and Co, 1933.

Heller, Milton F., Jr. *The President's Doctor, An Insider's View of Three First Families*. New York: Vantage Press, 2000.

Hoover, Irwin H. *42 Years in the White House*. Boston and New York: Houghton Mifflin Co, 1934.

Jaffray, Elizabeth. *Secrets of the White House.* New York: Cosmopolitan Book Corp., 1926.

Kirk, Elise K. *Music at the White House, A History of the American Spirit.* Chicago: University of Illinois Press, 1986.

Lathem, Edward Connery, ed. *Your Son, Calvin Coolidge, A Selection of Letters from Calvin Coolidge to His Father.* Montpelier: Vermont Historical Society, 1968.

____. *Meet Calvin Coolidge: the Man Behind the Myth.* Brattleboro: The Stephen Greene Press, 1960.

Lockwood, Allison.. *A President in a Two Family House: Calvin Coolidge of Northampton.* Northampton: Northampton Historical Society, 1988.

Longworth, Alice Roosevelt. *Crowded Hours, Reminiscences of Alice Roosevelt Longworth.* New York: Charles Scribner's Sons, 1933.

Marton, Kati. *Hidden Power, Presidential Marriages That Shaped Our History.* New York: Random House, 2001.

Moran, Philip R. *Calvin Coolidge, 1872-1933.* Dobbs Ferry, New York: Oceana Publications, Inc., 1970.

Murray, Robert K. *The Harding Era, Warren G. Harding and His Administration.* Minneapolis: University of Minnesota Press, 1969.

Parks, Lillian Rogers. *My Thirty Years Backstairs at the White House.* New York: Fleet Publishing Corp., 1961.

Randolph, Mary. *Presidents and First Ladies.* New York: D. Appleton-Century Company, Inc.1936.

Rogers, Will. *Letters of a Self-Made Diplomat to His President.* New York: Albert and Charles Boni, 1926.

Ross, Ishbel. *Grace Coolidge and Her Era, The Story of a President's Wife.* Rutland, Vermont: Academy Books, 1962.

Ross, Walter S. *The Last Hero: Charles A. Lindbergh.* New York: Harper and Row, 1964.

Russell, Francis. *The President Makers, From Mark Hanna to Joseph P. Kennedy.* Boston: Little, Brown and Company, 1976.

Seale, William. *The President's House, A History.* New York: Harry N. Abrams, 1986.

Seeley, Mary Evans. *Season's Greetings from the White House.* New York: a Mastermedia book, 1996.

Sobel, Robert. *Coolidge, An American Enigma.* Washington, D.C.: Regnery Publishing, Inc., 1998.

Starling, Col. Edmund W. *Starling of the White House, The Story of the Man Whose Secret Service Detail Guarded Five Presidents from Woodrow Wilson to Franklin D. Roosevelt.* New York: Simon and Schuster, 1946.

Stoddard, Gloria May. *Grace and Cal: A Vermont Love Story.* Shelburne, Vermont: The New England Press, 1989.

The Tercentenary Committee, *The Northampton Book*, Northampton: Alan S. Browne, 1954.

Timmons, Bascom N. *Charles G. Dawes, Portrait of an American.* New York: Henry Holt and Company, 1935.

Watson, Robert P. (ed.) *American First Ladies.* Hackensack, New Jersey: Salem Press, Inc., 2002.

White, William Allen. *A Puritan in Babylon: The Story of Calvin Coolidge.* New York: Macmillan, 1938.

Yagod, Ben. *Will Rogers, A Biography.* New York: Alfred A. Knopf, 1993.

Periodicals

Bittinger, Cyndy. "The Tiny Hamlet of Plymouth Notch Becomes Nationally Known During Coolidge Term" *The Vermont Standard*, October 30, 2003.

Coolidge, Grace. "The Real Calvin Coolidge: A First-Hand Story of His Life, Told by 50 People Who Knew Him Best And Edited with Comment by Grace Coolidge," *Good Housekeeping*, February-April, 1935.

Hennessy, M.E. *Liberty Magazine*, October 15, 1924.

Mercersburg Alumni Quarterly, Mercersburg Academy, Mercersburg, Pennsylvania.

Real Calvin Coolidge booklets, #1-17, Plymouth, Vermont: The Calvin Coolidge Memorial Foundation, 1983-2002.

The New England Journal of History, Volume 55, No. 1, Fall, 1998

ABOUT THE AUTHOR

Cynthia D. Bittinger is the Executive Director of The Calvin Coolidge Memorial Foundation where she developed the web site section on Grace Coolidge. She is on the editorial board of the journal *White House Studies* and wrote an article on Grace Coolidge for *American First Ladies*, a book with biographical essays on each first lady. She is a commentator for Vermont Public Radio. Her commentaries on Grace and Calvin Coolidge won an award from the American Association for State and Local History in 2004. She has taught Vermont History and Women in U.S. History for the Community College of Vermont.

INDEX

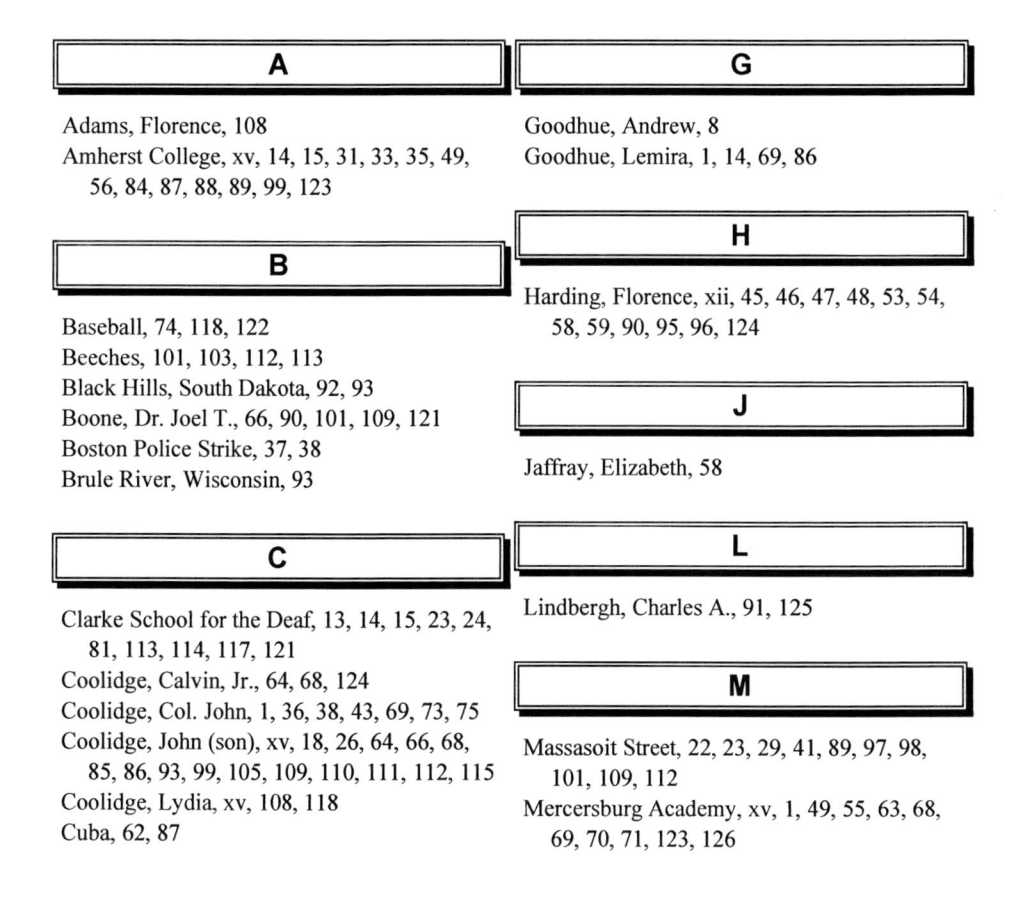

A

Adams, Florence, 108
Amherst College, xv, 14, 15, 31, 33, 35, 49, 56, 84, 87, 88, 89, 99, 123

B

Baseball, 74, 118, 122
Beeches, 101, 103, 112, 113
Black Hills, South Dakota, 92, 93
Boone, Dr. Joel T., 66, 90, 101, 109, 121
Boston Police Strike, 37, 38
Brule River, Wisconsin, 93

C

Clarke School for the Deaf, 13, 14, 15, 23, 24, 81, 113, 114, 117, 121
Coolidge, Calvin, Jr., 64, 68, 124
Coolidge, Col. John, 1, 36, 38, 43, 69, 73, 75
Coolidge, John (son), xv, 18, 26, 64, 66, 68, 85, 86, 93, 99, 105, 109, 110, 111, 112, 115
Coolidge, Lydia, xv, 108, 118
Cuba, 62, 87

G

Goodhue, Andrew, 8
Goodhue, Lemira, 1, 14, 69, 86

H

Harding, Florence, xii, 45, 46, 47, 48, 53, 54, 58, 59, 90, 95, 96, 124

J

Jaffray, Elizabeth, 58

L

Lindbergh, Charles A., 91, 125

M

Massasoit Street, 22, 23, 29, 41, 89, 97, 98, 101, 109, 112
Mercersburg Academy, xv, 1, 49, 55, 63, 68, 69, 70, 71, 123, 126

P

Pets, 77
Pi Beta Phi Fraternity, 2, 33, 37, 108, 123
Plymouth, Vermont, xiii, 1, 9, 15, 18, 22, 25, 38, 39, 41, 49, 50, 59, 64, 66, 71, 73, 75, 83, 92, 102, 103, 104, 105, 107, 109, 114, 115, 117, 118, 119, 120, 121, 123, 126
Prohibition, 46

R

Randolph, Mary, 59, 67, 84
Riley, Ellen, xvi, 59, 97, 98, 119, 120
Road Forks, 113, 116, 119
Rogers, Will, 90, 91, 124, 126

S

Stearns, Frank Waterman,, xi, 31, 123

W

White Court, 83, 84, 92
White Pine Camp, 84, 92
World War I, xiii, 2, 33, 35, 45, 78, 96, 114
World War II, xiii, 114

Y

Yale, Caroline, 13, 114